THE ELEVENTH COMMANDMENT

THE ELEVENTH COMMANDMENT

Transforming to "Own" Customers

Sandra Vandermerwe

For Internet web page please contact
Professor Vandermerwe at
http://www.demon.co.uk/vandermerwe

JOHN WILEY & SONS
Chichester • New York • Brisbane • Toronto • Singapore

Copyright © 1996 by Sandra Vandermerwe
Published 1996 by   John Wiley & Sons Ltd,
                     Baffins Lane, Chichester,
                     West Sussex PO19 1UD, England

                     National   01243 779777
                     International (+44) 1243 779777

Other Wiley Editorial Offices

John Wiley & Sons, Inc., 605 Third Avenue,
New York, NY 10158-0012, USA

Jacaranda Wiley Ltd, 33 Park Road, Milton,
Queensland 4064, Australia

John Wiley & Sons (Canada) Ltd, 22 Worcester Road,
Rexdale, Ontario M9W 1L1, Canada

John Wiley & Sons (Asia) Pte Ltd, 2 Clementi Loop #02-01,
Jin Xing Distripark, Singapore 0512

Library of Congress Cataloging-in-Publication Data

Vandermerwe, Sandra.
     The Eleventh commandment : transforming to "own" customers / Sandra
Vandermerwe.
       p.   cm.
     Includes bibliographical references and index.
     ISBN 0-471-95823-9
     1. Customer relations.   2. Customer satisfaction.   3. Customer
services.   I. Title.
HF5415.5.V358   1996
658.8'12—dc20   96-6473
                                                                CIP

British Library Cataloguing in Publication Data

A catalogue record for this book is available from the British Library

ISBN 0-471-95823-9

Typeset in 11/12pt Palatino by Dobbie Typesetting Ltd, Tavistock, Devon
Printed and bound in Great Britain by Bookcraft (Bath) Ltd, Midsomer Norton, Somerset
This book is printed on acid-free paper responsibly manufactured from sustainable forestation,
for which at least two trees are planted for each one used for paper production.

For my beloved daughters Emma and Meg

Contents

Preface

The ideas and concepts expressed in this book come from over a decade studying and working with different organizations, watching a new paradigm emerge and being made to happen by the men and women who run some of the world's leading corporations and institutions.

At the International Institute For Management Development (IMD), I was fortunate to be exposed to these individuals. From large, small, industrial and service organizations they came to Switzerland to share and learn, and in doing so both shaped and allowed us to help them shape their organizations to deal with the huge managerial challenges ahead.

Background to the Research

Part of the work for this book came from a research project which goes back many years, beginning in the days of the International Management Institute (IMI) – before the merger with IMEDE to become IMD, inspired by the then Director Juan Rada, who provided me with the support and intellectual energy I needed in the mid-1980s to begin to open up, explore and articulate new customer and corporate issues.

My research continued after the merger, culminating in several publications. Now this book is for practitioners and students with two major concerns:

The "Whys" "Whats" and "Hows"

One. If indeed sustained competitiveness is the quest, do corporations know how to "own" their customers now and in the future?

And two. "If not, why not", and "what" needs to be done to become a new corporation – one with whom customers do, want to do, and will continue to do business?

While I was writing the book, the if not "why" not; "why" is it important to radically change; "why" seriously focus on customers; and "why" this is different from what has been done before, became increasingly important.

Allow me to explain.

Most managers want to know the "how" – they are understandably impatient and want to get on and do things. Many have heard many concepts before – and the customer message is not new.

Part of my personal challenge, therefore, has and will continue to be, to get corporations, and the people within them, to understand that although the customer message is not new, change of such monumental proportions, both now and on the horizon, makes it almost impossible to answer (or even pose) new questions with old assumptions, beliefs and notions.

The existing paradigm must first be broken – people must first be made to feel and understand "why", without a profound understanding and commitment to what it takes to "own" customers, they, their organizations and even their industries are vulnerable – either they will disappear, or miss out on huge opportunities.

Only once people understand this "why" can an alternative representation of the world be offered on the customer corporate relationship, which is both understandable *and* do-able.

What The Book Sets Out To Do

This book tries to accomplish the following:

- Show why old ideas are still prevalent in organizations, what and where they are, and how to recognize them.
- Provide a new framework by which to focus on customers and take advantage of opportunities to add value – and then decide *who* does *what*, *when* and *how*.

Like many other contemporary writers in a variety of fields, I needed to express the paradoxes associated with the new corporate challenge, part of which is learning to work with ambiguity, and turn it to the corporation's advantage.

For example:

- Putting value in while simultaneously taking non-value out is a fundamental part of the transformation framework I offer.
- Working on twin tracks and managing at differing speeds in different parts of the organization, while complex, I try to demonstrate turns out to be more

practical than trying to do, achieve and finance everything all at once.

- Learning to work with structure and chaos allows for the flexibility needed to "do and learn" instead of waiting for data, proposals and long strategy documents that people feel they have to implement.

    My proposition is that transformation should be diffused through certain people within the organization who understand and are committed, and then influence "360 degrees" around themselves in order to make new behaviour the norm.

- Both routine and spontaneous behaviour allow the new organization to cater to individual customers and do so at low delivered cost with people in the organization able both to grow themselves and build the know-how base of the corporation.

I think it's a mistake to believe that once corporations take off their "blinkers" and learn what they have never known (or never had to know) they will be able to do a better customer job.

Not so simple.

First, customers don't know what they want – part of the challenge is finding new engaging ways to find out, so as not just to respond to existing markets and needs, but to lead and create those still emerging and those imagined.

A second point. Customers too are undergoing major change. The transformations I've described have been more like being "on the move with others also on the move" than having to change to a strict formula in order to meet fixed and predictable needs in the market place.

Though some customers will be adapting to changes more quickly than others, what they will all be looking for is a redefinition of the role of the corporations with whom they deal, one which will make better, simpler and more productive their personal and professional lives as they grow and develop – albeit into the unknown.

In this work I have tried to redefine what is meant by value and find some organizing frame which different institutions in various industry types at different points in the supply/distribution channel can *use and share* to profoundly "own" (and jointly "own") customers.

Redefining the Notion of Value

The premises are these:

- Whereas in the past we thought we were adding value, in fact often we were adding costs. Value only happens in the customer's space. What goes on in that space, i.e. what customers do to get the results they want, is what new corporations need to establish, and to these activities they need to learn to *add* value.

- Unless the value gets downstream to end-users everyone will ultimately fail. This being the case, all those involved in what I call new "competitive spaces" – built around customer activities – need to focus on the same thing and understand their respective role and responsibility, behaving as one from the customer's perspective, while each being best at what they do.

A large part of what creates value is the deep and ongoing interaction and relationship with customers. But we need to get beyond the solutions theme we took up in the late 1980s and early 1990s, and make the new corporation the "gateway" to an individualized set of solutions which gives its customers what they need to get the *results* they are after.

In the same way that this book asks managers to accomplish several things simultaneously, it tries to do the same – cover both the *substance* of what actually needs changing *and* the *process* by which the transformation is made to happen. (Most books on transformation or competitiveness talk about customer focus but don't go into any depth on how to achieve this.)

Articulating the New Terms and Tools

One of the reasons this book is able to offer a composite framework embracing both the "what" and the "how", is because the central organizing tool – The Customer Activity Cycle (CAC) – is process based.

So, it not only gives people a common language and grounding principle it:

- Helps people work together on neutral territory – all being concerned with end-user value.
- Offers a way to see, sense and concretely articulate the opportunities for putting value in, while taking non-value out.
- Stimulates questioning about the role of individuals and groups in the transformation and their behaviour, both internally and externally. It shows the implications for "who does what", "how", "with what enablers", making profits "from what", "when and how".

- Makes operational, projects which take the organization through the steps it needs to go, to build confidence and credibility.

Some of the questions in the chapters raise issues managers are only just beginning to battle with, so what the reader will find is often a description of a world still evolving.

Of course, being interested in learning from the experiences of corporations, I have used examples to demonstrate ideas and concepts in action, mindful that no two companies are ever the same, and that even if they were, to be ahead proactively, seeking to "own" customers, often means doing things without the comfort and certainty of knowing it has been done or worked before.

This book has been funded by IMD to whom I am grateful for some wonderful years of learning and for the opportunity to express my thoughts and ideas in the classroom and in several publications and cases. A special word goes to Xavier Gilbert for arranging the financing and support for this book.

Acknowledgements and Thanks

Of course it is impossible to separate one's own ideas from those of others. I see this book as a synthesis of what is known and has been written about by authors – many of whom well known – as well as the ideas and experiences of managers who, as they experiment, learn and express what they are thinking, feeling and doing, create the future for us to make some sense of.

My exposure to colleagues around the world and their writings has given me the foundation and points of departure which no doubt the reader will recognize in the chapters. I have, to my knowledge, given credit where due, and added some interesting works as supplementary reading.

Unless otherwise stated the information in the book comes from interviews. The interpretation remains my own.

In my previous book *From Tin Soldiers to Russian Dolls – Adding Value Through Services*, I took a decision not to mention any executives by name to protect their privacy. Here I have decided to refer to the individuals involved – I hope I have reflected their ideas well and done them justice.

Hundreds of interviews have made my work possible, and I have not been able to mention everyone by name.

To the men and women who have supported me over the years I am deeply grateful. I hope they know how much the academic world depends on them for generating, articulating and testing the knowledge and ideas that will hopefully lead to a better world for us all.

Also significant in this book is my work consulting with firms and institutions and my thanks goes to the many executives who have shared with me some of their most exciting and daunting times and provided me with material to use.

Marika Taishoff has worked with me for several years and many of the case studies mentioned have been co-authored with her. She also helped me compile the bibliography. Others I would like to mention are Michel Zurich and John Evans and their colleagues in computers and at the IMD library, and Max Thomen for his help with the figures.

Who can write a book without the love of those around them? Once again I'd like to record how much I appreciate the extraordinary resilience and unfailing support of my family: André my husband, and our two fabulous children Emma and Meg.

SECTION 1

MAKING THE PROACTIVE LEAP

I don't believe in circumstance. The people who get on in the world are the people who get up and look for the circumstances they want, and if they can't find them, make them.

George Bernard Shaw

CHAPTER 1

Knowing How to "Own" Customers

What we've learnt over the past decades is that the most important capability a corporation needs to have is knowing how to "own" its customers.

Everything else follows.

Some people object to the use of the word "own" (they say you can't/shouldn't try to own anyone).

True, but I like it because it says exactly what we are trying to achieve.

It's very effective in pushing us to think beyond historic notions of customer satisfaction and ask what we must become good at, now and in the future, to sustain the kind of market power that will both attract and hold this generation of customers and those to follow.

The notion of "owning" customers is a way of thinking about the market place and about the people with whom we work to create value. It's about how people talk (and what they talk about) and how this translates into a specific pattern of behaviour and action, which the customer experiences through our products and services.

During a transformation people need to think about how they think and how this may limit their organization's ability to excel in a changing market place.

They see the need to radically change their assumptions about success, and make the needed adjustments in their behaviour, so that their organization can become profoundly customer driven.

Rather than just be more proficient at making and moving more products or services to meet year-end budgets, people learn how to develop and build relationships, which commit customers to do business with them over a lifetime.

From these relationships, they become the "gateway" to the solutions individual customers within chosen markets need, in order to get the results they want in their daily work and private lives.

With customer "ownership" central to a transformation, the interests, language and ideas from people from different parts of the organization are able to converge and see common threats, opportunities and challenges.

And no one can hide.

People begin to acknowledge that the only way forward, of benefit to all stakeholders, is one which proactively pursues ongoing value for customers.

The question then is: how to make it happen.

CHAPTER 2

Don't Miss the Moment

We now live in a permanently and continually changing environment.

One which needs to keep destabilizing if it is to keep innovating and progressing.

Given the far-reaching implications of this, it is only those corporations able to continue to drive forward into unknown futures that can continue to be out front, securing a sustainable competitive position.

The assumption I'm making is that right now for most, a bold leap from where they are – and have been – to where they need to go is an inevitable first step.

As Andrew Grove of Intel once said in an interview with *Fortune Magazine*:

> "There is at least one moment in the history of any company when you have to change dramatically to reach that next level of performance. Miss the moment, and you start to decline."

When he made that remark Intel had already become a huge success story. Having sensed in the 1980s that mainframes – the product for which it had actually been created in the first place – had to go to be replaced by microprocessor chips for the new emerging PC market ("big machines don't need to think for computers, small chips can do the job for customers"), Grove began a transformation to make his corporation into an international superstar.

Market minded Bill Gates of Microsoft too seized the moment at that time. While IBM continued to automate factories, making machines with better functions and commands, Gates pushed to make PCs for users, putting his effort into the design of the intelligence and graphics ("real people like colour and graphics") instead. In retrospect, Grove and Gates were both revving up for a future they not only saw but were themselves about to make happen.

As their experience continues to show, a bold leap is a necessary reoccurring step for sustaining success.

Determined not to be swayed by market upheavals, Gates and Grove zoomed ahead into new and unknown terrains in the 1980s, resolved to ride with breaks in the environment rather than be submerged by them. They thus changed not only their corporations, but also the rules for being and staying in the game.

Now, a decade later, with the global electronic web and a truly universal standard a reality – where the software may come for free and the money from a service through the Internet on any electronic appliance – Gates, who at first demonstrated limited interest in the Internet, says he intends to keep Microsoft ahead – becoming the Internet software market leader and standard setter – by providing integration and continuity between the "web" and the PC.

> "Death can come swiftly to a market leader", he says in his book *The Road Ahead*, published late in 1995. "By the time you have lost the positive-feedback cycle it's often too late to change what you've been doing, and all the elements of the negative spiral come into play. It is difficult to recognize that you are in a crisis and react to it when your business appears perfectly healthy. That is going to be one of the paradoxes for companies building the information highway. It keeps me alert. I never anticipated Microsoft's growing so large, and now, at the beginning of this new era, I unexpectedly find myself a part of the establishment. My goal is to prove that a successful corporation can renew itself and stay in the forefront."

Begging the Big Questions

But many firms miss the moment. How come?

Addressing the Symptoms

As Gates and others have said, they actively seek to protect the status quo for as long as possible rather than abandon the comfortable and familiar.

They thus tackle a whole lot of symptoms rather than root causes.

Fortunes are spent on initiatives which improve existing processes, and make changes in bits and pieces of the organization, rather than taking the bold leap needed to get the fundamental shift to create something new.

The big questions are left begging.

A classic mistake is for corporations to decide it's now they must change and quickly restructure, for instance.

But restructure around what?

Until decisions are made about what markets the firm wants to target as its "own" (and, often more painfully, which they intend to eliminate), no amount of restructuring can help.

> "Rather spend the time, energy and money on figuring out what it takes to become or stay a customer focused company", says Jon Hargreaves who successfully led Northumbrian Water through a customer driven transformation in the mid-1990s. "Restructuring won't make people's behaviour entrepreneurial, and what will cannot be put onto an organizational chart."

Many other initiatives out of context beg the real customer questions and hold up moves to seriously drive a corporation to the market.

Benchmarking is an example.

It assumes that there is a precedence somewhere for excelling at something that has to be done. But this often stalls breakthrough change, especially if we are dealing with futures yet to be discovered. What corporations need to do is encourage experimentation so that their employees actively look for exciting new ways to deal with customers, rather than emulate what's gone before.

Re-engineering is another popularized tool which, if disconnected from what management is trying to achieve in the market place, can do more long-term harm than good.

Eager as they are to do things better, cheaper and get quick results – easy to measure and communicate – managers miss the moment by moving into programmes like re-engineering without addressing the real questions such as:

- Where are our greatest threats, opportunities and challenges likely to come from for the year 2000 and beyond?

And

- Do we have a (common) view of how our markets may evolve, be influenced and change in the future?

- What emerging new trends can we foresee (or do we intend to create) which may change the way customers operate, buy and/or use our products and services?
- Who could take our customers away from us? Where is the real competition likely to come from and why?
- What is it we should be good at in the first place?

The Problem With Success

It's now history that being strong in mainframes, IBM's management kept on going in the same old way in the 1980s. They got into PCs late and, when they did, decided not to make the investments needed in software and operating systems to help get value down to end-users.

IBM's Folly and New World Wisdom

That IBM was late in making the needed changes – from product to market, from corporation to customer – cost them dearly.

But it's only one illustration among many of a failure on management's part to leap at the correct moment into the new world.

IBM's problems made world headlines because they were big and high profile. But there are several firms and industries who didn't or still aren't moving, or aren't moving as dramatically or rapidly as they should.

They make the assumption that because they are doing well at one moment they will automatically be carried successfully into the future.

The reason is quite simple to understand – at all levels in an organization it's much easier to convince people to change when things are not going well or when the signals for change become obvious, than to get them to throw away what seems to be working.

And that's of course what's got to change.

Only when the losses piled up did the real energy begin to flow and new customer values become articulated as a serious part of IBM's plan.

And therein lies an important learning.

While it's easier and sometimes quicker to get people to undergo change when things turn bad, the recovery process is much more difficult. There is always a heavy penalty to pay – market image will be damaged, funds will be short, confidence will be low and the organization will be laden with a lot of the wrong kinds of skills.

Success can (and does) breed failure. The better the blinder so to speak. Success obscures from our vision the first signs of failure. It can make us complacent and insensitive to danger.

The better a corporation becomes at doing something the more difficult it is to do something else.

So they wait for a crisis.

General Electric's (GE's) Jack Welch – whose great achievement was to have recognized in the early 1980s when he became CEO and then again in the 1990s the radical changes GE needed and make the courageous moves (despite having been scoffed at) – says:

> "When it's been so easy for so long, some people can never get around to facing reality. That's why you see so many businesses making incremental changes when they get in trouble: they can't believe that the situation is probably ten times worse than they've admitted to themselves."

Who said success shouldn't stop us from worrying?

Today's change leaders must consciously and continuously be poking and provoking their organizations, challenging what is now working well.

This doesn't mean throwing everything good out. On the contrary it's important to know why you've succeeded.

But it does mean that what has been successful in the past probably won't work in the future. (The corollary is worth thinking about too: what has not worked in the past may very well work in the future!)

Chapter 3

Assessing Yourself on the S Life Cycle Curve

The classic sigmoid (S) life cycle curve (see Figure 3.1) is not new but it continues to help managers learn through a graphic framework.

You will notice there are three points on the S curve. This is intended to make some generalized distinctions so

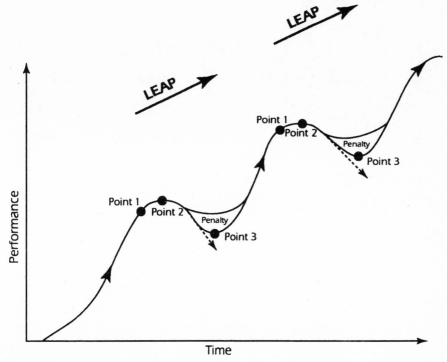

Figure 3.1 The Classic S Life Cycle Curve

corporations can assess where they are along the curve and, given what they are doing (or not doing), where they may be headed.

At *point 1*, nothing or very little will yet have happened or impacted to sound the alert. On the contrary a corporation will still be on the up. Nonetheless, it will be clear (to someone at least), that the moment has come to make a leap.

If a firm waits till *point 2*, they will be reacting to outside forces and the signals will be more obvious.

Any company near or at *point 3* will already be in crisis – the longer they wait, the heavier will be the penalty (see figure).

Mark the sketch with an X to show where you think you are. Try comparing this with what others in your organization think.

Ideally the juncture at which to leap is somewhere between points 1 and 2.

As we've discussed, the secret is to start a new S curve (there will be several of them) before the previous one peters out.

CHAPTER 4

Defining Your "Market Space"

Old indicators or concepts can be dangerous in the world
in which we now live.

For instance, many firms are still obsessed with market
share. Deep down they believe if their market share is OK
they are OK.

The Pitfalls Of
Market Share

Spend a moment asking yourself: what is market share
anyway? Does it exist?

Share of what? Rank Xerox were looking at copiers
when they defined market share in the 1980s and early
1990s. But at the same time that they were saying to
customers "make one and photocopy the rest", Hewlett
Packard (HP) was saying "make as many as you want
with our printers".

As the Rank Xerox and HP example shows, one of the
greatest pitfalls to using "market share" is that definitions based on traditional product/markets miss the real
question: who is the competition?

Market share is a statistic which means nothing unless
we know the boundaries, i.e. "market space", we are
talking about.

Though market share may lead to economies of scale
which contribute to a corporation's competitiveness
(more later), it does not, in and of itself, make a
corporation competitive on a sustained basis.

Here are several good reasons why it is not a reliable
indicator for the "market power" new corporations need
if they are to "own" customers:

1. They may be getting an increasing share of a shrinking
   end-market.

2. Market share costs money, especially if competitive strategy is based on selling only products *or* services – the so-called "core" items that increasingly can be copied.
3. Market share is a lag statistic: it does not tell a corporation a thing about its capability to "own" customers in the future.
4. It also doesn't tell it how well it did with its customers in the past – i.e. it says nothing about the quality of customer relationships.
5. Market share doesn't tell a firm how many unhappy customers it has.
6. Or how many it lost and has had to replace, and what it cost to do so.
7. It doesn't tell firms about customer usage (they may have the product but may not be using it enough or they may be using someone else's, as happened in the credit card industry).
8. Or tell a company how it is doing against firms outside its industry who may be its biggest rivals for customers' "ownership".
9. Or whether it has satisfied, loyal, repeat customers or customers coming and going or switchable.
10. Or whether the corporation has the "correct" customers. (Who would have gone out of their way to get Microsoft as a customer ten years ago?)

"Market Power" in New "Market Spaces"

The boundaries between "market spaces" are what distinguishes one opportunity from another. Within this "market space", firms either learn to do the things that differentiate them from others, or they end up selling on price.

In orthodox marketing we talked about "push" (getting goods through channel members to end-users) and "pull" (creating demand in end-user markets through various creative tools, thereby generating the demand.

Not enough, the new corporation has discovered to maintain long-term customer relationships.

What they need is the capabilities to build the kind of "market power" which will give them 100% of the market(s) and spending, inside the "market spaces" in which they decide to do business.

New corporations discover "market space" by:

- Creatively rescoping what it is that customers do/ could do to get (and continue to get) the results they want (more later).
- And reframing this around a descriptor, thereby defining the territory in which both customers and firms serving them operate/could operate.

The following chapters will elucidate.

SECTION 2

LOOKING BEYOND WHAT YOU CAN SEE

The real voyage of discovery lies not in seeking new landscapes but having new eyes.

Marcel Proust

CHAPTER 5

Managing the Not-So-Obvious

Despite Winston Churchill's remark, it's difficult to look further than you can see, being proactive about customers means looking for, and at sometimes obvious, data and signals and arranging and reading them in a not-so-obvious way.

Some firms and industries suffer because managers continue to fool themselves that because they have all the market studies and hard statistical evidence they "know" about customers.

Opportunities are lost time and time again because they are "looking" at historical data, products and segments rather than what is to come.

The classic marketing textbooks told firms to find out what customers want. They said market research would get the facts about customers (true). But they assumed that these facts would predict future customer behaviour (wrong).

Customers Don't Know What They Want?

The most sophisticated of market research cannot forecast real life customer reaction with any degree of accuracy.

Customers cannot easily express what they may or may not want in products and services, or how they intend to behave in a world they have not yet experienced.

This doesn't mean that they won't respond, offered something that provides added value to their life and work.

Internet (owned as you know by no one) is poised to change the lives of tens of millions of people by the year 2000. It came about because a group of American academics wanted to talk to each other. On to this network the US military added their electronic connections.

Since then organically (and unpredictably), Internet has extended itself – grown by the people who want it.

Go back.

When Walter Wriston, ex-chairman of Citibank, did the original research for Automatic Teller Machines (ATMs) which no one had heard of then, the data the results brought in was a big negative – he proceeded any way. When Akio Morita of Sony researched his idea to make a Walkman, the feedback he got was "no one – male, female, adult or kid – would buy a recorder that couldn't record".

Ask yourself what sort of response would 3M – who now demand, by the way, that 25% of every unit's sales must come from products introduced within the past five years – have got if they had seriously tried (they didn't) to research whether people would buy (use, pay for and become addicted to) little pieces of yellow paper (Post Its) "that stick but don't stick".

The point is that there are serious limitations to what existing data from traditional techniques can tell you about customers. Most of the information we get is history anyway by the time we get it.

New corporations therefore talk about leading the public with new products and services rather than asking customers what kind of products or services they want or would buy.

They acknowledge that people don't know what is possible. So they are empathetic rather than definitive about markets – intuitive rather than just analytic.

Being prepared to imagine markets and offerings that don't yet exist for and with customers that can't necessarily express what they want in traditional terms, means moving forward on many fronts without all the data and feelings of certainty we had in the past.

This does not exclude getting feedback from customers – provided it's the feedback we need to know.

Much of the research and feedback up to now has been through aggregated figures from structured questionnaires telling us about "average" feelings from "average" customers.

We now need specific feelings from individual customers about their particular experiences expressed in their own unique way.

Keep the emotion, language and narrative in the feedback if you want to know how customers feel, say many firms. Stories, expressions, metaphors and discussion will tell you a lot more than the hard facts.

New corporations driving to the market place talk to customers – both internal and external. They get impressions rather than average statistics – they want to know how customers feel about them and the individuals to whom they are exposed.

Dissatisfaction With Customer Satisfaction Data

Curiously, concepts like customer satisfaction, which occur after the fact, have lulled firms into a false sense of security about their relationship with the market.

One reason is that often data is related to static criteria like the attributes or features of the product and services (easy to measure), instead of the overall customer experience.

And short-term customer gratification, which we now know is not necessarily indicative of a customer's long-term commitment.

In fact, statistics from the United States show that between 65% and 85% of customers who switched automobile brands said they were very satisfied. Satisfaction scores averaging up to 85% to 95% while repurchase rates average only 40%.

Interestingly, committed customers tell you when they're dissatisfied. When the relationship is good and trusting, you are the first to know if there is a problem and recovery is part of the ongoing connection.

However, experience shows that it's not what firms do, as much as what they are *not* doing that makes customers potential switchers – ready to move if they find an alternative supplier.

General reluctance by firms to look outside their immediate business into a new "market space" has had profound long-term implications.

It goes back to a whole mental framework which in the past prescribed sticking to "core" business which was interpreted as "keep doing what you do best better".

The difference now, is that we broaden the "core" to include everything the customer needs to get a result.

And if we can't do it, we either learn how, or find partners who can.

Let's go back to Northumbrian Water. They received a letter from Ford Motor Company – a standard letter sent to all the water companies – asking them whether they would be interested in managing Ford's total water

Northumbrian Water's Leap

activities in the UK. A carefully worded "thanks but no thanks" letter was drafted by them to Ford. Said one executive at the water utility:

> "Water management wasn't our core business. We were good at getting large quantities of water to factories and collecting and treating the sewage and waste to very high standards. So we said 'no' to the opportunity to work with one of the biggest companies in the world!" (Note: it takes 30 000 litres of water to build the average car and 8 pints to make 1 pint of beer!)

At the time, Northumbrian Water had one of the highest service quality ratings in the industry for drinking water, with compliance levels of 99.8%. In many instances it had been transporting and treating drinking water and waste water for individuals and companies for 25 years without receiving a single complaint.

Oticon Brings Customers In

The new corporation sends people out to be with, observe and talk to customers, because the best ideas come from being with and thinking like customers.

New corporations also bring customers in.

Oticon – which moved from a traditional product to a customer driven corporation in the early 1990s – brings the elderly and deaf into their head offices in Denmark.

Commented Lars Kolind, the CEO:

> "As part of the transformation I wanted to have real customers right in the heart of our business. So we created clinics at head office where customers come and talk and are examined and are helped by our product development, engineers and servicing people.
>
> At the beginning it was a shock for us to see deaf people in our marble reception halls.
>
> But it was an important step in the breakthrough because customers became a visible and physical part of our day-to-day activities."

CHAPTER 6

Demystifying Marketing

Strange as it may sound, marketing – or management's interpretation of it – has been one of the most serious barriers to "owning" customers.

The notion of having to focus on customers was correct. What went wrong was that corporations expected marketing to be solely responsible for the relationship between corporations and customers.

It never has, nor will it ever be remotely possible to have one link between a firm and its customers. No one function – call it what you like – could or can be responsible for "owning" the entire customer relationship.

Furthermore, many corporations constructed themselves in such a way that marketing was kept separate from day-to-day operations in the market place.

This proved fatal to customer relationships because often, while it was marketing and sales with whom customers had closed the deal, the ones they saw the most – and indeed often only saw – were the operations people.

In other words, marketing was responsible for the promise, while operations was responsible for the delivery (or non-delivery) – and the twain often did not meet.

Worse still, "customer services" – out on a limb somewhere – was responsible for cleaning up the mess.

Aggravating all of this was the passion and push for getting as much volume sold as possible.

This led to several creative ways of "broadcasting" corporate and brand virtues to sell more, rather than encouraging genuine dialogue between the customer and corporation and monitoring the results customers were getting.

A firm has to sell, of course. But who sells what, how much, to whom over what period of time, with what partners at what return, are the real issues with which new corporations must now wrestle (more later).

The Economics Of Customer Retention

The notion of "economies of customer retention" has captured the imagination of scholars and practitioners alike.

Recently Bill Gates said:

"Microsoft has got to get most of its revenue from repeat customers rather than new ones. That's a fundamental shift in our business model and we have to start to change ourselves, our products and our strategies now to be able to do that."

To "own" customers means replacing old notions of making and moving as many "core" products or services as possible and instead keeping customers as long as possible.

The reasons are simple:

1. The longer customers stay the more proportionately they are likely to buy and recommend.
2. The more you sell to the same customer, the less it costs you.

The price of a lost customer can cost huge amounts in time money and effort. Figures vary depending on the industry: Hewlett Packard (HP), who also made the bold steps before being hit by major upheavals, estimates it costs five times to attract a new customer as it costs to keep an old customer – and some consider that figure conservative for their own industry.

CHAPTER 7

Finance Baffles Brains

Throughout the 1980s and into the early 1990s, IBM's financials looked excellent; revenues almost trebled from $23 to $63 billion between 1979 and 1989. Profits were growing: it remained the market share leader in each of its computer businesses, with the highest market value and strong ratios.

Until net income fell in 1989 when management responded by an attack on costs. 1990 was a very good year – profits were up 60%, and revenues 63%. An extension of the mainframe range, "the most important new product introduction in 25 years", led to predictions of even larger revenue growth.

Despite massive restructuring efforts and cuts in operating expenses, in 1991 IBM reported its first ever real loss. Then in 1992 followed the biggest loss ever in US history.

What went wrong?

Among other things, IBM thought it was leading in the leading markets: in fact, if it was leading it was doing so in the shrinking markets.

Its relationship was with products, not customers – it was afraid to switch from one product to another for fear of cannibalization.

Like others, IBM scrutinized and crunched out the numbers. Management continued to cut costs going into major restructuring – whereas what IBM needed was much more radical.

When still being run by an analytic bias, management takes a narrow view of reality. Historic (hard) facts overrule intuitive or creative feelings about market position.

In these types of organization, conventional accounting and financial measures assess the corporation's performance as a snapshot which shows only what is brewing on the surface and what has been accomplished in the past.

Conventional ratios are compared to others *inside* the industry whereas what we now know is that competition for customer "ownership" is much more likely to come from *outside* traditional borders.

SECTION 3

REVERSING THE LOGIC

If you don't change the direction in which you are going you might end up where you are headed.

Old Chinese Proverb

CHAPTER 8

The Linear Trap

New problems cannot be solved by old notions.

This chapter examines linear thinking so popular and successful in the last decades, and presents a framework for implementing an alternate customer philosophy, for now and our times ahead.

One which seriously begins with the market and then decides on appropriate action – who does what, where, when and how.

Late in the 1980s DuPont was shocked to find sales dropping in some of their historically strongest European markets.

It had the largest market share and the best technical products that money could make.

What had gone wrong?

Research done by DuPont – renowned globally for grafting powerful brand images on to constantly improved industrial products (think Teflon, Lycra, Stainmaster) – revealed the following: when planning a home, customers left the purchase of a carpet to last: curtains, furniture, hi-fi equipment and white goods took priority. Customers enjoyed buying holidays, PCs, cars, clothes – you name it. But not carpets: these they went looking for only when they had to, and reluctantly. Repurchase cycles went up from an average of five to 12 years – increasingly customers were being enticed to buy other floor coverings, such as wood, marble or tiles.

"We hate buying carpets", they said.

You might argue that this is a very specific case: an industrial company far removed from the end action in a mature market. But let's take a closer look.

The DuPont Carpet Fibre Case

We have a well-known corporation doing everything conventional wisdom taught yet the market was disappearing before their very eyes. Though the product was industrial, it was destined for people like you and me who experience frustration at the end of the trail every day of our lives.

DuPont did something about it (which we will come to) and turned what could have been a disaster into a great coup (although the idea Jim Carr and his team proposed was deemed to be sacrilegious at the time!).

Who was to blame for the deterioration is the interesting question? Carpet fibre producers? Processors? The carpet manufacturers? Wholesalers, distributors, retailers?

The logic was to blame – linear value chain logic around which all our economic, managerial and financial systems were designed in the industrial economy and which has programmed management to think in a sequential way too literally for much too long.

Is Linear Logic Dead?

Linear logic was invented for machine-like product and service settings, where offerings could be controlled and inputs and outputs were precise and predictable.

Quite different from the flexible spontaneous products and services we now need in order to "own" customers.

With linear long and standard runs paramount, what corporations loved most were large, mass standardized orders and the customers which provided these.

But these customers were often not the profitable ones.

And the push for discounts to get orders, squeezing suppliers, adversarial dealing, cherry picking and the like which became the hallmark of relationships between members of the distribution chain didn't get the benefits to customers that were intended.

The SKF Story

When Maurice Sahlin, now retired as CEO of SKF, the Swedish global bearing manufacturing giant, realized that although everyone and everything had been concentrated on the large Original Equipment Manufacturers (OEMs) supplying the mass standard orders, this wasn't where the profits were coming from.

The after market – which *used* equipment – was where the real opportunity lay, he had declared. Any delay or downtime cost these customers plenty, and what they wanted were services to avoid this happening, for which they were prepared to pay.

A radical customer-driven transformation then began, which was to become a model for corporations world-wide.

Ever heard of the Jiffy postal bag? It's made by a medium-sized UK packaging company which, among other plastic and paper products, produces a cushioned padded envelope which has become a household name.

Jiffy Packaging Puts End-Users First

Upon his arrival at Jiffy in 1991, Peter Lewis found a typical volume-based product-focused organization (selling 40% of the UK's protective packaging through distributors and subdistributors). His object was to make Jiffy proactive and customer based.

Typically, like SKF, Jiffy had always regarded distributors as *the* customers.

End-users were an amorphous mass "out there somewhere", with whom they had no or little contact. Characteristically, the linear chain functioned on pushing products through the system, based mainly on specification and price.

But as one Jiffy executive so clearly put it, from the end-user's point of view, this made no sense:

> "Bulk packaging cost money to store. As well, since packaging was such a minute part of overall expenses, end users didn't take it very seriously and often made bad application decisions.
>
> But so often if package decisions were poor or a shipment badly packed, millions in damage (reputation, time and hard cash) occurred."

Pushing for volumes through discounts resulted in some cases in chaos in the market place. HP found in the early 1990s that because distributors and value added retailers (VARs) had different starting prices, retail price wars raged. End-users got cheaper prices but not necessarily value because services so crucial to make HP products perform were often ignored or done poorly.

HP Pushing Value Through VARs

Today, like others, HP are doing away with discounts based solely on volume.

By contrast, value is shared with VARs so as to get sustainable loyalty from chosen end-user markets, with the emphasis on jointly aiming for and "owning" these markets.

This is what leads to the desired flow of orders over lifelong periods which captures the economies of retention we talked about earlier, rather than just the economies of scale which ended in discount wars.

In this view of the world, customers get better "bottom line prices", and better results over the period of use rather than just a one-off cheap transaction.

Boxes And Arrows

Linear logic assumed that one thing followed another in a particular order and so long as this happened, we got a predictable result.

Flows and activities were put into boxes with arrows in between to show how value was accumulated within a firm's supply or distribution chain.

Goods (products or services) supposedly acquired the value internally, by moving along this sequential chain from one box to another, i.e. through R&D sourcing, production, sales, logistics, etc. (see Figure 8.1).

Or externally, down a channel from one part of the supply/distribution chain to end-users (see Figure 8.2).

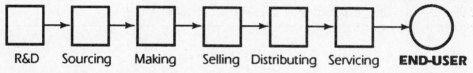

R&D   Sourcing   Making   Selling Distributing Servicing   **END-USER**

Figure 8.1   The Traditional Internal Value Chain (Simplified)

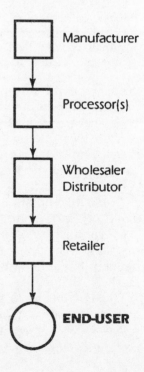

Manufacturer

Processor(s)

Wholesaler
Distributor

Retailer

END-USER

Figure 8.2   The Traditional External Value Chain (Simplified)

What an item was finally worth was assumed to be the accumulation of what went *into* making and moving the goods (products or services), getting them down these linear chains into the final market place.

In fact, this proved not to be the case.

CHAPTER 9

An Alternative Customer Logic

There is another logic afoot in new corporations, which I call reverse logic, with a growing awareness that:

- It was costs, not necessarily value, that were accumulated along the classic linear chain.
- The mere existence of a company, supplier or distribution chain did not guarantee value to end-customers.

This forward–backwards or reverse customer logic can be captured in three basic principles:

Principle 1
Unless value is getting downstream to end-users, neither corporations nor industries can sustain their competitiveness.

Whether we are pumping and distributing oil or gas, underwriting complex insurance policies, or making carpet fibre, PCs, or cookies, unless someone at the end of the line – however long that line may be – is getting value out of these products and services, and is prepared to pay for this, we will find ourselves out of business.

This eliminates once and for all the notion of each party in a distribution channel positioned in a neat series, doing its own thing.

And the assumption that customers are the ones next in line, and that that is the end of the line.

Remarked David Whitwam, CEO of Whirlpool, the North American appliance manufacturer, in a *Harvard Business Review* article:

"Until you stop thinking about the retailer as the customer and start thinking about them as part of the process, you're going to be delivering the wrong kinds of products.

Sears Roebuck is a great example. We developed products to sit on their floors in competition with other products that were sitting on their floors. If they said 'I want this washing machine with three whistles and two bells, and we want it to be pink', we gave it to them. Little did we know that the customer didn't want machines with whistles.

Today we don't treat each other as customer/supplier. We see ourselves as partners trying to solve a common need."

The Trouble With (Only) Branding

Branding is no substitute for getting value downstream. It is indeed an effective way to create presence and image, in order to attract a particular group of customers.

But corporations fall dismally short when they assume that getting creative "pull" through branding and advertising is enough to retain lifetime customers.

"It's not the people (we sell to) who pay our invoices", said Intel's Andrew Grove, "but the end users of PCs whose minds we have to win in order to succeed." (Note how effectively Intel has used consumer branding "Intel Inside".)

Late in 1994 his statement would stand the real test when the "Pentium" chip crisis hit. At first Grove argued that it was a small and rare technical problem – not an issue end-customers should be concerned about. Then he retracted his words, and the chips.

(The share price went up that day by $3.06!)

Principle 2
Only when thinking starts with end-users, and works back into the organization, can we hope to "own" customers.

Corporations thus need to develop new methodologies for sensing and anticipating end-user patterns, interpreting and translating what is currently unknown or unseen into opportunities for ongoing market and corporate growth.

New corporations go into the market to find out about end-users, even though they may be far removed from them on the traditional distribution chain.

This was one of the first moves Peter Lewis made when he arrived at Jiffy – the company having previously relied exclusively on distributors for information and feedback.

How did end-users feel about packaging? Did they know what to use and when? Were the products available giving them what they wanted?

Who were "they" anyhow?

Without "knowing" exactly what to expect, Jiffy targeted some of the growth end-user markets. Among others the company looked at mail order (the largest user of postal bags) and found that no one in the industry was providing an offering suited for their special needs (e.g. flaps, labels, weight protection, reuse features, etc.) for the mailing of products such as videos and cassettes and disks.

Principle 3
New corporations go forward, then build organizaions and skills back from customers, and up to top management; rather than move forward and down from top management into the market place.

Organization structures as we've known them, driven from and to the top, neatly verticalizing and delineating turf and tasks, are overturned to build organizations capable of discovering and delivering customer value, when, where and how it needs happening.

Retailing, at the end of the linear chain, also needs to embrace this forward–backwards principle.

Focusing Retail Forward– Backwards

For though retailers have had direct contact with end-users, often attention has been on their internal procedures, with head office dominating decisions and culture, rather than their end-users.

One example: Mr Minit, which has a stronghold of 1200-odd retailers worldwide and which, among other things, repairs shoes and makes keys, decided the time had come in the early 1990s to make a switch.

Previously all attention had been on head office – what they had to know. The shops were quite literally "outlets".

Head office knew everything, but only about what the shops were achieving financially, not about what they were doing with customers.

A lot of information was coming in, taking massive amounts of time and energy but none of it told them what they really needed to know – what did customers want?

With new customer logic, distribution channels are also built back from the end-user market place, to achieve one cost effective system dedicated to discovering and delivering customer value (more later).

In the traditional linear model, the bits of the distribution chain haggled over margin. This is what was seen as being "competitive".

In the new view of competition the question is: how does the system as a *whole* create and deliver the maximum value-add to end-customers in the most cost effective way?

Sequential linear value chain building blocks are replaced by dynamic interlinked processes that begin with a definition of this end-user value and what needs to be done for and by whom within and across companies and industries.

To get the value downstream means choosing and bringing together corporations which share common customers in one value-creating community, which jointly seeks to "own" defined end-user markets – rather than just selecting distribution which gets rid of high volumes of product.

Choosing Partners at Oticon

When Oticon, the Danish hearing aid manufacturer, made its move to focus on end-users, Lars Kolind included only the most professional hearing clinics and hearing aid dealers in the world.

"Until 1988 our strategy was to be the biggest and best and to do everything for everybody. Clearly this didn't work for us. So in 1989 we refocused our business towards those dispensers or retailers who were most concerned about their end users. That was – and continues to be – the basis for all reductions and changes."

Their 100 dealers and distributors are all involved in product development today, spending time at head office in Denmark.

Similarly, Oticon personnel are out there with dealers and distributors, observing them at work and discussing new ideas. "Keeping physically close to them is a part of the strategy to work jointly to serve end users", says Kolind.

Discussions are purposefully about business issues around joint customer "ownership" rather than audiological talk.

The DuPont Carpet Fibre division worked on exactly the same principle.

Starting with end-user markets, they chose carpet manufacturers, wholesalers and retailers with whom to work on "enhanced flooring covering" products and services.

Together they defined markets such as hospitals, hotels, etc., and worked out a joint approach to "own" these markets. Then they decided on the relative roles and responsibilities of each entity.

In this sense, partnering means living a common need for a common market in a common "market space".

The main driver becomes merging capabilities to discover and deliver the customer value, and relooking resources so as to avoid waste and duplication.

Included in this is joining infrastructures and technology with other members of the channel, combining expenses and saving costs by eliminating unnecessary controls (e.g. double checking), duplications (e.g. warehousing or sales) and erroneous efforts not leading to downstream value (more later).

CHAPTER 10

Mindsets: The Enemy Within?

More than anything else it's the mindset – the programmes deeply ingrained within each one of us – that
determines how we think, talk and behave.

Mindsets reflect not just our view of the world, but the
shared views within the organization built up over
generations.

More powerful than structures or systems, they forge
the set of individual and collective beliefs and assumptions that guide people at all levels in what they have to
do in order to succeed – both internally and externally.

The linear value chain mindset, which goes from head
office to retail, manufacturer to distributor, R&D to
logistics and services, is so deeply entrenched in
conventional management that it takes conscientious
effort to make a switch to the reverse customer logic.

To change mindsets, they must first be brought to the
surface.

Not just because top management need to know them,
but because if people's behaviour is to change they must
have an opportunity to understand, question and
challenge their existing beliefs and actions.

Questions such as these need to be discussed:

- What do I think is important, and consequently what
  actions do I prioritize?
- What are my assumptions about customers and
  success and how do these influence my decisions on
  what to do and how to work?

Comparing Linear and Customer Logic

It never ceases to amaze how corporations which declare they must focus on customers tell managers to get on with it and are surprised when nothing happens.

Consciously, people must be made to see the limitations of the mental model they are using and the impact of it on their behaviour if the long-term competitiveness of the corporation is to be achieved.

For their behaviour to become profoundly customer centred, they have to believe they have to behave differently – as well as why.

They must see the reasoning for change, see the reasoning behind the new customer direction and understand the new world view put to them.

And they must be excited by what they see and hear.

Table 10.1   Comparing Linear and Customer Logic

(Linear) Logic	*(Customer) Logic*
Our part (function/division/department/ unit/country) matters most	The good of the whole matters most
We therefore strive to retain our independence	We must therefore actively work towards interdependence and reciprocity
We are responsible for doing our own function/division/department/unit/country activities as well	We are jointly responsible for activities which create and deliver value to customers
Some people are not connected to customers	Everyone is connected to customers – either external or internal
We serve customers who are next in line in the distribution chain	We need to focus on end-users, if we are to "jointly" serve our customers
Our aim is to get "high volume" unit sales	Our aim is to deliver ongoing "high value" to our customers at low delivered cost
We get information on end-user market from distributors/retailers, brokers, etc.	We individually and jointly get, and we share information on end-users
Our responsibility ends when we sell customers in the channel the product they want at a competitive price	We need to share roles/responsibilities with others in the distribution channel, so that end-users get the results they are after
The object is to sell high volumes to get economies, thereby making profit targets	The object is to optimize the operations of the whole distribution channel so that everyone will be successful
We need to compete both internally and externally to compete	If we don't learn how to collaborate, we can't sustain our competitiveness

Only once prevailing mental models surface and people can openly discuss, ask questions and become influenced by those around them, has the transformation process has begun.

In Table 10.1, are some of the differences between linear (backwards–forwards) and customer (forewards–backwards) logic.

It's worth explicitly comparing this linear and customer logic to get a common understanding of the differing values and behaviours they enshrine.

It inevitably raises the issue of how the institution has operated in the past, and what is now needed to be done differently.

SECTION 4

MOVING MINDS TO MARKETS

*One doesn't discover new lands without consenting to lose
sight of the shore for a very long time.*

André Gide

CHAPTER 11

Managing Transformation as a Process

You will remember that we talked about the S curve and the need for an institution to leap at the correct moment – somewhere between points 1 and 2 – rather than wait for stagnation or a crisis.

Because traditional logic is accustomed to reacting to something specific, rather than proactively anticipating without the obvious signs or an impending disaster, people often need to be made to feel a sense of urgency.

Urgency, because unless a way of thinking about and handling customers noticeably different from the past is found, the firm will lose its competitive position.

This sense of urgency comes in the first of three identifiable phases in customer-focused transformation.

Phase 1 is a period of *agitation*, when people begin to "see" things differently, having been made "uncomfortable" about the present way of doing things.

Phase 2 is a period of *education*. Here a new customer framework and common set of terms and tools becomes the glue which binds a new purpose, people and the new projects that will take the company into its future.

Phase 3 is when *integration* takes place – customer principles and behaviours become firmly embedded in new working practices, and new role models displaying new behaviours aimed at discovering and delivering customer value become institutionalized as the norm.

The Three Phases of Transformation

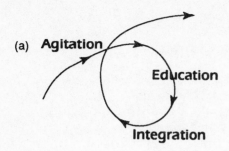

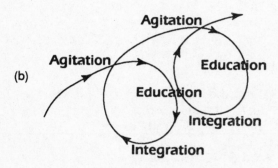

Figure 11.1   Phases In The Transformation Process

The three phases are shown in the Figure 11.1a.

On the one hand, each phase needs to happen to make the next feasible.

But as Figure 11.1b shows, the phases are fluid and reiterating, more like a spiral than a closed loop – transformation being a cumulative, overlapping and reinforcing process, happening at different times and speeds in an organization (more later).

In the first phase of the transformation the object is to make enough people feel agitated enough, that in the future either their corporation won't make it, or will miss out on huge market opportunities unless radical changes are made.

I call this agitation "strategic discomfort".

The Sun Life Assurance Case

One example: early in the 1990s the new CEO of Sun Life Assurance, John Reeve (he has since left) – having joined the company a year before – set about making some serious changes in the way the company dealt with its customers.

Within just a couple of years, the company rose from 11th place to become the 4th largest UK pension, life and investment company, winning several awards for service quality and performance in Europe.

A deliberate move to shake things up and create a shock wave through the corporation was taken by Reeve initially, so that people were made alert and ready to make the necessary adjustments as the transformation progressed.

"People had never had to fight for business before at Sun Life. Some who had been there 20 years or more couldn't believe it when the announcement came that overheads had to be reduced by 20%–40%", said Les Owen, then Chief General Manager, now CEO.

The Sun Life experience is classic.

Creating "strategic discomfort" is easy enough when the signs are already obvious – be they external forces or deteriorating results.

But when signals are not obvious or are due further into a future still to occur, they are more difficult to articulate and communicate.

To make the signals tangible in some form and format so that people will understand and react in the appropriate way, change leaders must:

- Sense the signals – finding them – asking where could they come from? What could they be?
- Interpret the signals in a creative way – translating them into meaningful patterns, threats and opportunities for the corporation.
- Communicate them in a message understandable to those who matter (more later on this) – checking to see whether they have heard. Do they know what it means? Have they accepted it?

Arenas, Agendas and Actors

All the companies I've studied and worked with have made the leap with the help of some initial "thinkout" sessions.

A forum is needed over and above the normal routines and strategic planning function and events.

Questions such as these need time to be thought through in a creative way:

- What are the potential converging forces which would radically change our business?

- How could converging technologies change what people buy, how, when and from whom?
- What would our role be in these scenarios?
- Can we visualize who the competitors might be and how they would behave?
- What could they do for customers that would be dangerous for us?

"Thinkout" events usually include a combination of the following techniques:

- Discussions/exercises – to agitate and stimulate debate and get people into a common world view and frame of mind.
- Revealing analyses of data – organized differently to show a different picture of the present and future.
- Scenario building – classic "what ifs" and brainstorming.
- New ways of defining/viewing/mapping markets/customers/competition.
- Surveys to highlight/substantiate problems/opportunities/challenges.
- Customer face-to-face discussions or electronic communication to the group.
- Creative gap analysis comparing capabilities for past results and future goals.

From the "thinkouts" should come strong commitment from a coalition of people dedicated to make the transformation work, preferably with some specific agendas.

Price Waterhouse Enters a New Era

Balancing what fits with what people can understand and accept, and finding ways to show that what fits what they understand and accept may not take the business into the future, is an essential part of these thinkouts.

This includes making triggers substantial enough to galvanize attention, energy, resources and future initiatives.

Nothing was surprising about what Price Waterhouse, operating in 120 countries, discovered in the rigorous positioning exercise they did in the early 1990s to assess their global competitive strength – they were undifferentiated in the customer's eyes.

But what the exercise did was to get a common top management view of the problem around which they could build and communicate a vision for a new global professional services institution.

Communicating triggers in a creative way can speed up strategic discomfort and accelerate buy-in.

The various factories in the Minit group in Europe, for instance, were producing a larger and larger variety of increasingly expensive products such as fixtures, shoe repair and key cutting machines, and rubber for soles and heels. But the shops either didn't want them, or found they could be bought cheaper locally.

How to get the message across swiftly and dramatically to factory managers was an important part of the transformational challenge. A showroom (which had to be 80 square metres to accommodate the over 800 items) made the point memorably.

Each product was displayed with the price: light grey for Minit's goods; blue for those other retail competitors were using; and yellow for what was being locally purchased by Mr Minit's stores (the metaphor used for the warehouse design was a "toy shop").

Factory managers were able to see immediately, in a way and at a rate that could never have been achieved in the normal manner, that too many things were being made too expensively, and not being bought by the local shops.

Additionally, within a couple of hours of conversation, ideas and know-how on how to solve the problem were exchanged.

Mr Minit's Creative Strategic Discomfort

Everything we've discussed so far (and will continue to) has language implications. What people think, feel, what they prioritize and why, is revealed in the language they use, and in the way they communicate.

Language Talks

Words, concepts, metaphors and symbols are therefore important motivators and compasses for transformation. (If you ask in the traditional way, expect traditional answers.)

Expressing in words and pictures what traditional language couldn't, was the upside down pyramid which Jan Carlzon, ex-CEO of Scandinavian Airline Systems (SAS), made famous: 15 years later corporations are still using it.

So was the "experimental group" which Jurg Chresta, CEO of Ciba Geigy Allcomm, used to get a market-driven spirit and culture built for the new communications group (previously the internal advertising service) for the global pharmaceutical giant.

Or the "spaghetti organization" concept expressing a new way of working for customers at Oticon, invented and implemented by Lars Kolind.

Discussed throughout this text will be the significance and techniques of reinventing a new and common glossary and a set of concepts and terms, as a way to fuel and focus a customer-driven transformation.

Quite simply, it helps to communicate the message and provides a concrete lever for getting people into a single frame of mind and mode.

Looking back at their experiences, several change leaders I've encountered say a new and consistent set of terms enabled people, who previously may not have had much to discuss, to communicate with each other in a way which would have been impossible before.

CHAPTER 12

Faulty Assumptions and False (Slow) Starts

Here are the several faulty assumptions which can damage or slow down a customer-focused transformation (see Table 12.1).

They will be discussed as the issues in the chapters unfold.

Table 12.1 Faulty Assumptions and False (Slow) Starts

Old Assumptions	New Assumptions
We don't need a vision till we've got a strategy	We need a vision to give us direction – strategies will then evolve
We can only move with consensus from the top	We can move with consensus where we need it and get the other people to follow
We should start small and see if it works	We must transform the way we behave and make it work
The problem is with some parts of this company – we need to fix those first	We need to touch on all parts of the company to make this really work
We can't move because we don't know what to do	We must move and we will learn what to do as we go along
We can't give too much time and resources to this	We must give our time and best resources to this
How can we do this and keep the business going?	We have to do this and simultaneously keep the business going
Let's find out what others in the industry are doing first	Forget others in the industry – we want to be ahead
We must move slowly so as not to cause instability	We must move quickly or our situation will become instable
Our people will never understand and accept "this"	Our people are all consumers – so why shouldn't they understand and accept this

CHAPTER 13

One More Time: Why Visions (Whatever You Want to Call Them) Do Matter

Top of the list of faulty assumptions is that a vision isn't necessary. This view can seriously delay a transformation's progress. (IBM's CEO Lou Gerstner first said "no vision needed", then retracted his words.)

"Strategic discomfort" is achieved through agitation. It is deliberately aimed to destabilize. The wake-up call – if it doesn't happen nothing else will.

But with too much agitation, for too long, without some tangible direction, there will be the kind of fear and instability which leaves people hanging, insecure and confused.

At Sun Life the initial shock grabbed everyone's attention. But it wasn't fear that pushed the transformation through, recalled Les Owen.

Very quickly people were bought into the customer way of thinking by seeing that both the company and they would be better off with the newly stated vision.

"It was this that gave and sustained the momentum that changed Sun Life", Owen recalled after reflection.

The notion of a vision has been well enough covered by the literature not to have to go into great detail here.

Except to say: sometimes a vision is what triggers the transformation and it is what causes the strategic discomfort – other times the realization that there is no vision is the detonator.

Vision can be the inspiration of one person who sees and expresses a private dream about a world to come –

or building a vision can be the first part of a process of getting common understanding and commitment from members of the coalition.

Vision Drives
Reverse Logic

A good vision gives new possibilities and substance to a future yet to be achieved by the firm transforming.

People say visions must be achievable. But at the start, who knows what's achievable?

Who could have imagined that British Airways, bottom of the pile when Sir Colin Marshall declared his vision in the early 1980s, could ever become (can it stay?) "the world's favourite airline"?

Or that the metal slab that sits in the gardens of Microsoft Way – the corporate main offices of the Microsoft Corporation in the forests of Seattle, USA, expressing Gates's vision of "getting a computer onto the desk of every person in every home" – would become a reality by the year 2000?

Or that by 1995, with technology dramatically changing from desktop computing to information highways, Gates would admit that what people need is access to the correct information highway, which may (not if he can help it) make the PC incidental?

A good vision forces people inside an organization to look at themselves and their personal goals – they have to be able to identify with it, stand by it, defend it, get excited by it and make it happen.

A good vision is also a unifying force for building a new corporate way, illuminating the way ahead for the people who have to decide what to do – and what not to do.

Visions With
a Noble
Intention

Also, a good vision has a noble intention.

New corporations which successfully take us into the future will be those striving to better the general well-being of the human condition.

- Today AT&T sees itself as an "enabler of human contact" – thanks to its technology, people don't have to feel isolated or be alone, they say; customers have easy access to each other and the services they need across the world.
- Matsushita's vision is to "enhance the physical, mental and spiritual well-being of people".

    Their object is not just to create the best electronics in the world, but to help people around the world in their work and home lives, making them feel less threatened, afraid and vulnerable. Technology is not only to stimulate and enlighten, therefore, but to help

individual people feel safer, calmer and more re-
assured about the things they do and need.
- Oticon's vision is "the provision of quality of life for
  people with impaired hearing – so they can live the
  way they wish".
- Baxter Health Care USA is intent on giving patients
  better "managed health care". Working with and
  through the hospitals, their aim is to make products
  and services which lead to "accelerated comfort and
  healing" for end-user patients.

Industries have visions too. And, increasingly, these must
seek to improve the world, the way people work,
communicate, live and learn
   Explaining this as part of his "network centric
computing vision" for the new IBM (where instead of
power going into the mainframe or PC, it goes into the
network into which customers have access) at the
Comdex computer show in Las Vegas in November
1995, Lou Gerstner talked about the need for corporations and industries to look at the broader implications of
the futures they are creating and to respond to the total
needs of society and their customers.
   At the same conference (and in his book mentioned
previously) Bill Gates expressed the same sentiment.
   Despite concerns (such as individual privacy, commercial confidentiality and national security, pornography
and intellectual property theft) which require serious
reflection and management by both corporations and
industry, the information highways will, he believes,
potentially build a better world which:

> ". . . will enhance leisure time and enrich culture by
> expanding the distribution of information. It will help
> relieve pressures on urban areas by enabling individuals
> to work from home or remote site offices. It will relieve
> pressure on natural resources because increasing num-
> bers of products will be able to take the form of bits
> rather than manufactured goods. It will give us more
> control over our lives and allow experiences and
> products to be custom tailored to our interests. Citizens
> of the information society will enjoy new opportunities
> for productivity, learning, and entertainment. Countries
> that move boldly and in concert with each other will
> enjoy economic rewards. Whole new markets will
> emerge and a myriad of new opportunities for employ-
> ment will be created."

CHAPTER 14

Making Missions Market Making

Where there is a market or potential market there is a mission.

And where there is a mission there must be a purpose.

Again, a lot has been written about missions. Without getting into the semantics and debates on preferred terminology, missions are not visions: missions follow the vision. They give a corporation a reason for being.

They lie somewhere between the articulation of the vision and what has to be done in order to occupy a particular "market space". They are thus a powerful link between the agitation and education phases of a transformation.

To be more explicit:

Vision articulates what an institution wants to *be*.
Missions state what the firm intends to *do*.

Good missions achieve two seemingly conflicting objectives simultaneously:

One, they push boundaries to reveal new "market spaces" where the customer operates and needs to be served
And two, they focus strategies, because they frame these new "market spaces".

In other words market making missions define, but don't confine.

Here is an example. In 1993, the Chairman of Rank Xerox, Paul Allaire, led the transformation of the firm through yet another S curve.

He redefined the mission as "document management" ("if you see your documents differently you'll see your business differently", he said to customers).

Rank Xerox's Mission: "Document Management"

The corporation used this as a powerful transforming lever in the emerging global networking "market space" to differentiate itself from previous eras in which the boxes (mainly copiers) were the mainstay of their business.

First, Allaire had to position the document (print and/or electronic) as *the* important asset in home and work productivity.

Instead of the document remaining a commodity in the customer's eyes, the object was to demonstrate it as the knowledge base of the future, valuable especially in a corporate context for gathering, recording and disseminating vital ideas, know-how and information.

The document had also to be positioned as a valuable (if not the only) communications device, between people working together and between institutions and their customers.

Good
Missions
Are . . .

From a good mission everything follows:

- Decisions on resource allocation
- Redeployment of people
- New product and service innovations
- New capability building
- With whom to partner
- Where and how to generate profit

But what makes a mission good? Here is a list of 12 criteria.

A good mission:

1. Has integrity – a true sense of purpose – something the corporation intends to do and deliver better than anyone else.
2. Has a distinguishing notion (a good mission can be stated as a story or a slogan) – something which makes it unique and gives it a distinctive position in the chosen market(s).
3. Should be meaningful and relevant – and make a tangible difference to personal and/or work lives.
4. Is enduring and extendable, is able to sustain relationships.
5. Communicates easily and memorably – encapsulating both a purpose for the firm and a promise to customers.
6. Is simple (as opposed to simplistic).
7. Is grounded in values with which employees can associate.

8. Is easily translated into specific behaviours – from a good mission, employees should know what to do differently, or what different activities to do.
9. Is distinctive – it is memorable and "new/novel", not only gets people pointed in the same direction, but energized.
10. Is credible but not confining – capturing competencies the corporation either has or has the potential to quickly acquire.
11. Pulls together resources from various parts of the company.

Going back to SKF for a moment, what industrial after-market customers – such as steel, textiles and paper mills – wanted was a lot more than bearings.

Bearings versus Trouble-Free Operations at SKF

Goran Malm, who led the Industrial Services division (he has since left), came up with "trouble-free operations" as the mission.

Very quickly it fuelled the transformation. It excited customers, employees and distributors alike. Here was a whole revival in thinking and operations encapsulated in one statement. It became the unifying instrument that everyone could understand and relate to, bringing together the various parts of the organization.

Said Malm at the time:

> "After-market expertise, experience and skill were scattered in islands throughout the company. I knew I had to find something which could pull it together, something which made sense to customers and staff. But we had never talked about tangible benefits for our customers before – how they could actually save time and money. We only discussed quality and the price of the bearings.
>
> Now we had something to talk about that was of relevance to us and the customer, from which we could grow customer relationships, revenue and profits and, most importantly, our own capabilities."

12. Market making missions are also human. They are conceived by people (us) for people (us). They should link humanity with functionality.

Linking Humanity and Functionality

Part of the Rank Xerox mission, for instance, is to make the lives of individuals easier, not just more productive. (Did you know that the average office worker in the US spends four weeks or more a year waiting for the correct documents to be found?)

Bringing stress levels down and easing the whole machine–human interaction is an integral part of their ideas about what "document management" can do for people in their personal and professional capacity.

Aptly, say two professors specializing in competitiveness, Gary Hamel and C.K. Prahalad, in a passage from their book *Competing for the Future*:

> "Corporate leaders must never lose the ability to identify with the individual stranded by a defective car, too busy to wait in a long queue, unable to 'phone home' from a distant international locale, or trying to feed and clothe a family on a tightly stretched budget. If senior management isn't capable of empathizing with the needs of 'ordinary' customers it will be incapable of meeting those needs ahead of competitors."

SECTION 5

BECOMING THE "GATEWAY" TO CUSTOMER SOLUTIONS

Probable impossibilities are to be preferred to improbable possibilities.

Aristotle

CHAPTER 15

Redefining Value

In my last book, *From Tin Soldiers to Russian Dolls*, I wrote about tribal folk describing objects in terms of what function they serve rather than what they "are".

A tree, for example, is described by them as a source of nourishment and protection. A room where people work and live. A bowl holds liquid while the carved rim encircling the bowl decorates.

In other words, each part is described by what it does – i.e., the "verb" rather than the "noun".

There is nothing quite so effective as getting people within a corporation to start talking "verbs" instead of "nouns", in order to show the difference between what they are selling and what customers are buying.

Talking Verbs not Nouns

Thinking and discussion soon go off the "products", i.e. – loans, PCs, insurance policies, copiers, pesticides – and on to the market.

People begin to see the obvious: nouns soon become commodities. Whereas it is the verbs that carry the code for discovering and delivering customer value add.

From this comes the mission.

Table 15.1 gives some examples. All of them have or will be discussed in the following chapters.

Ironically one of the most serious drawbacks of sticking to the nouns and defining a corporation in these terms is that it can seriously limit product innovation.

Had the telephone utilities of yester-year thought in terms of "mobile communications", "office liberation", "mobility" or "independence" for, say, emerging virtual sales teams, they may not have allowed the now

Table 15.1 Comparing the "Nouns" to the "Verbs"

The "Nouns"	The "Verbs"
AT&T Lines and Phones	Communications/Connectability
Baxter Healthcare (USA) Drugs and Medical Equipment	Patient Healing and Comfort
Ciba Geigy Crop Chemicals	Safe Crop Protection
Citibank (Consumer) Loans, Credit Cards	Total (Global) Banking Experience
Oticon Electronic Ear Hearing Aids	Lifelong Hearing
DuPont Carpet Fibre	Enhanced Floor Covering
Matsushita Home Electronics	Human Electronics
Nokia Cellular Phones	Mobile Communications/Freedom/Mobility/Independence
Rank Xerox Photocopiers	Document Management
SKF Bearings	Trouble-free Operations
Whirlpool Washing Machines	Total Fabric Care
Zurich Insurance Insurance Policies	Risk Management/Asset Protection

successful Nokia – then an obscure Finnish company – to take hold of the alternative office "market space" through cellular phone technology.

Had they become masters at connecting people, instead of just lines and cables, they may have asked: do managers need phones anyway and thus got themselves into alternative solutions ahead of others in the information networking highway battle?

Of the global appliance industry, David Whitwam of Whirlpool explains that thinking has been so narrowly focused on the machines instead of the fabric-care that there has been little radical improvement in appliances in the last 30 years.

He described their strategy now as:

"Going beyond traditional product definitions we are now studying consumer behaviour from the time people take off their dirty clothes at night until they've been cleaned and ironed and hung in the closet. What are we looking for? The worst part of the process is not the washing or drying. The hard part is when you take your clothes out of the dryer and you have to do something with them – iron, fold, hang them up. Whoever comes up with a product to make this part of the process easier, simpler or quicker is going to create an incredible market."

What the telecommunications and appliance examples show is the growing awareness that new corporations need to redefine value in terms which reflect improvements for customers, instead of only for the products or services.

Consider these examples.

Matsushita found that a large proportion of its Japanese customers were getting inferior listening performance from their increasingly superior video and TV products.

Matsushita Acoustics and Japanese Customers

Why?

They were buying machines that were too big for the size of their rooms; they were not maintaining them well enough; and incompatibility between curtaining and carpet fabrics and acoustic technology adversely affected the sound quality.

Despite buying good lubricants, Northumbrian Water was spending lots of money on downtime delays, shortened life of machines and time wasted because its engineers were having difficulty lubricating the pumps needed to move water supply and sewage. (Did you know that 70% of all machine failures in the UK are due to poor lubrication?)

Lubricants for Utility Supplier Customers

Here were some of the reasons engineers gave: machine suppliers put oil into the pumps, which could not always be mixed with other lubricants in stock; tins were difficult to open with consequent mess and wastage; difficulty was experienced getting oil out of cans into pumps, and dirt in cans led to contamination.

Ciba farmer customers in parts of the US were buying the best chemicals that machines could make for weeds and pest elimination. But while pesticides got rid of the bugs farmers were not necessarily getting a safe crop. Other plants were being affected by the pesticides which killed off the next season's production.

Ciba Geigy's Pesticides for US Farmer Customers

Bally Suisse
Shoe
Customers

Bally, the international shoe company, was one of those which had waited until their performance had begun to stagnate before taking the leap.

When Stephano Ferro came to Bally in 1992 he found a company still faithfully following a culture based on making and selling shoes.

What customers had been getting were products that bore testimony to the long-time skill of the shoe craftsman.

What Ferro had to do was radically change the firm so that customers got the look, feel and wear they wanted, to get the results over the lifetime of the shoes – what he called "total footware performance".

Hypotheses for Customer "Ownership"

What this amounts to is the following.

From a customer's point of view, value is not what goes into products or services.

Value is what customers *get out.*

They get this value out *over a period of time*, rather than at a point in time.

What we should have done in the past to better describe economic value was to look at the proper utilization of products and services.

Productivity would then have been a measure of the improved and increased value customers received, instead of the number and cost of making and selling extra units.

This leads to at least two hypotheses for customer "ownership":

1. You can put as much *into* a product or service – if customers don't get the value out you will never make them lifelong investments.

And following from that:

2. Increasingly, a firm's ability to "own" a set of customers depends on its ability get value *out* of products and services for customers, rather than just put and sell more improved versions of them.

CHAPTER 16

The "Gateway" Paradigm

Which brings us both to (and beyond) customer solutions, discussed so much recently.

What does providing solutions truly mean?

First, it means companies are selling "applied performance" rather than just products or services.

Which in turn means they and their partners are responsible for getting a defined result.

The first time I encountered the phrase "applied performance" was at a workshop in Geneva when a senior executive from Grace Chemicals was expressing the difference between selling specialty chemicals and delivering solutions to their customers.

This is how he put it:

> "Customers don't want specialty chemicals (to treat their water). They can get that from one of several suppliers. They want to turn on the tap get the correctly treated water at the correct time and price in the correct quantity at the correct temperature."

From specialty chemicals to shoes all the examples we've discussed are saying the same thing: it's the results or outcome customers get from products and services rather than the products and services, i.e. the inputs that create the value.

In this view of the world, utility and application are more important than the items themselves.

Solutions become the demand side of performance.

And corporations which can get a set of solutions to customers, to produce the desired and long-term customer outcome, become their "gateway".

"Gateways" do the following which makes them different:

- They proactively anticipate and push for new opportunities for customers, as opposed to reactively only solving problems.
- Through them the various solutions are channelled and flow – they add their value to produce a total result for customers.
- They connect and integrate the various solutions, not just inside their own corporations, but between themselves, other companies and industries to produce a total customer experience.
- They become, therefore, the powerful "centre" for the customer value-creating and delivery system, not just the dominant (dominating) member of a linear supply and distribution chain.

New corporations become "gateways" because they extend their thinking and capabilities beyond making and selling what they do best (better).

They "see" new "market spaces" and concentrate on building capabilities to provide the value add potential within them.

And what they can't do themselves, they get done.

Here is an example.

Total Care at Zurich Insurance

Rolf Huppi masterfully led the global transformation at Zurich Insurance – a challenge which began in the early 1990s and continues to break ground in countries all over the globe.

"The Zurich" he describes as an integrator and contributor to people's lives – at work and at home.

> "We continually ask ourselves: how can we be a part of customers' daily lives – what we call 'total care'. Making relationships with customers more meaningful and helping them with the unforeseen is our key task today.
>
> When there is a problem we want to be there (first) to help. If something goes wrong in the home we want to take the first steps. If a pipe bursts we want to (or get someone to) clean it up – generally help the customers to protect and manage their assets whether or not it involves a claim.
>
> In fact the claim is secondary."

Total care, as Huppi explained it, is not just related to the insured assets because customers have needs outside of that narrow focus. Any problem, emergency or accident at home or in a foreign country, or help or advice needed

Table 16.1 Moving Through the Stages to "Gateways"

Stage 1 → 1960s	Stage 2 → 1970s	Stage 3 → mid-1980s	Stage 4 + mid-1990s
value= features	benefits	solutions	*"gateways"*
offering= product or services	products augmented by services	products and services	*"products" of the products and services*
object= market share "boxes"	market share products	market share products software and services	*market power in new "market spaces"*
market power= sell "boxes"	help customers make better documents and make documents better	help specific user groups to use documents better and differently	*become the integrator of improved life and business performance through documents*

by customers in protecting or managing their assets, are provided – either executed by Zurich themselves or found by them and delivered by others.

Table 16.1 tracks the journey from selling the product or service to becoming a potential "gateway", using Rank Xerox as a working example to demonstrate.

Rank Xerox as a Working Example

Rank Xerox is making the transformation needed to be able to connect the various solutions that go to make one ongoing experience for customers by creating, distributing and communicating documents around the world through its own and others' products and services.

Looking at the table you will see that none of the stages exclude the others.

That is:

- *Features* of the basic product or service have got to be there, constantly improved, based on ongoing learning. (Stage 1)
- *Benefits* for specific groups of customers are necessary depending on specific user needs. (Stage 2)
- *Solutions* should be customized to solve specific user group's problems. (Stage 3)
- And all of the solutions need somehow to be linked into one integrated *"gateway"* result (Stage 4)

For example: Rank Xerox and AT&T have developed a distribution and print-on-demand system.

Features include security, file storage and status checking (giving permission for access to buyers).

Benefits range from reduced warehouse and shipping cost, to small investors now being able to avoid huge investments in private infrastructures.

Solutions are customized for specific sender and receiver user groups – from students to software houses.

Into the global offering go the various solutions to form a "gateway" – software, distribution, shipping, storage, printing, binding, etc. – that ultimately produce a result for people both sending and receiving documents in the form they require, when and where needed.

On Becoming a "Gateway"

Becoming a "gateway" entails these fundamental principles:

1. Understanding your role in relation to others in getting the value to end-users.

For a company like Rank Xerox this means articulating the role of "document management" – in, say, a bank, tax authority, insurance company or aircraft manufacturer – in the protection and transferring of ideas, information, intellectual property and know-how to help these firms compete more effectively.

Take another simple example. Sun Life found that part of the delay getting the OK to people wanting life cover was due to hold-ups on the part of so-called third parties such as doctors, accountants, other insurance companies or brokers. A large part of this was obviated by reducing the complexity of their documents.

2. Being prepared to influence and collaborate so that other products or services used by customers are interconnectable and interoperable.

As we saw from the Matsushita, Northumbrian Water and Ciba Geigy examples, a lack of compatibility between products and customer usage made getting value out to customers impossible.

The superior Matsushita video equipment couldn't produce superior sound because of the textiles used by carpet and curtain manufacturers; the engineers couldn't mix the lubricants or get them easily from tins to the pumps so they ended up frustrated and delayed; the farmers had problems getting safe crop performance and ongoing productivity, due to mixes working for some aspects of the crop but killing off others.

Louis Gerstner, who took the reins of IBM in 1993, as the first non-IBM chief executive is trying to get common standards in the computer industry.

The industry still doesn't work to make things easier for customers, he admits. His personal experience is testiment to this – he once commented that he has eight computers in his office and every one turns on differently and boots up differently.

The new corporation increasingly sees itself as one of a total package of events that goes to make the overall customer experience. And it proactively pushes for the whole result rather than its own small bit.

For instance, knowing that their pesticide chemicals are only one of many that go to make a totally integrated solution for farmers in the USA, Ciba Geigy now provide a "tank mixing" system. Items from different manufacturers can now be mixed and made to work together optimally.

3. Being prepared to sell less of what you were good at making and moving in the past, and more of what makes customers good at what they do.

In efforts to become a "gateway" through superior water and water treatment management, Northumbrian is working with key corporations to increase their market performance through better, more cost-effective and environmental products and processes, rather than just trying to get them to buy and use more water.

In some cases this may mean helping to reduce corporate water bills.

4. Knowing, understanding, and – when applicable – recommending, selling and maintaining competitive products and services.

For the automotive after-market, SKF provides kits – which include up to 15% of bearings SKF purchases from competitors.

Additionally, the kits contain several products from other manufacturers, e.g. seals and gaskets put together specifically for each of SKF's 8000-odd distributors in Europe, depending on the dealers and end-user markets for whom they cater.

5. Doing things for customers – before rather than after the fact.

Remote diagnostics versus repair is probably the example cited most obvious.

But in a world dedicated to achieving real customer value, the notion of preventing rather than curing can go a lot deeper.

For example what if: pharmaceutical firms were judged, not on how many pills doctors prescribed, or how many pills people swallowed, but on how many "well" customers they had (as Chinese doctors are) and on the caring for and getting patients through the various stages of their lives?

Or life insurance companies were judged on whether people lived longer/better rather than how quickly claims were met? (Aegon in the Netherlands pays a premium to people at a certain age if they are healthy.)

Or insurers prevented accidents instead of selling more policies to cover accidents? Zurich Insurance go into retail stores and factories and ask: what causes the millions of small incidents that could lead to small accidents that could lead to the bigger ones and ultimately to the disasters? How can we help customers prevent them?

Or lawyers were rewarded not for winning a case but for how few clients had to go into litigation?

Or auto dealers made money not on how often or well mechanics fixed cars, but on how seldom it was needed?

SECTION 6

BEING ALL THINGS
TO SOME PEOPLE

The business of everybody is the business of nobody.

Lord Macaulay

CHAPTER 17

Reconfigurating the Market

Corporations who used linear logic tended to categorize customers into two camps – "those all the same" or "those completely different from each other". They responded accordingly by *either* differentiating their "product" *or* going for a low cost strategy.

New customer logic accepts that customers are *both* the same *and* different.

Its object is to deliver high value to customers within given markets *at* low delivered cost.

This chapter presents a model for reconfigurating the market place using the new customer logic.

It begins at level 1 on a familiar note – "massification".

But here's how it is different from Ford's famous "any car as long as it is black" line – which first directed, then misdirected managers.

Being All Things to All People

Rather than assuming customers are all the same, it begins by acknowledging that there are generic needs *common* to all customers, which need to be articulated if economies of scale are to be found.

These generic customer needs (see x axis in Figure 17.1) become the *mass* component of the offering (see y axis).

And economies become a function of customer demand as opposed to corporate supply.

New corporations move to the next level in the reconfiguration model. The questions are: what are the target segments within this common mass who share *similar* needs? (see axis x of Figure 17.2) and what part of the offering needs to be *targeted* for them? (see axis y).

Being Some Things to (Only) Some People

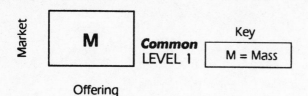

Offering

Figure 17.1   Reconfigurating the Market

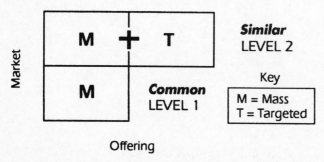

Offering

Figure 17.2   Reconfigurating the Market

Here the model progresses from "being all things to all people" to "becoming some things to (only) some people" – the chosen target segments.

Summing up the argument for market segmentation:

- Without choice there can be no purpose.
- Without purpose there can be no mission.
- Without mission there can be no definition of the market.
- Without a definition of the market there can be no segmentation.
- Without segmentation there can be no distinctiveness.
- Without distinctiveness there can be no competitiveness.

Breaking the Paradigm With Market Segmentation

While market segmentation is not new, it's amazing how even today many corporations still don't give it the attention it deserves.

New corporations, having come from high volume industrial cultures, quickly learn to use segmentation to focus and drive their transformation – especially at its initial stages.

Before setting out to build and execute strategies, they ask: what markets do we want to "own"?

In the face of commodity price wars and deregulation, with the all-too-familiar, off-the-shelf massified insurance products (such as property, motor and accident) being pushed out into the household and corporate market place, Rolf Huppi used market segmentation to break the old paradigm at Zurich Insurance.

Three years subsequent to the start Huppi had this to say:

> "Getting people to see that there were different customer segments was the single most important decision we made. It forced us to understand the workings of our business better and ask ourselves whether we had changed, and what we needed to gear ourselves up to genuinely become customer focused."

There are important principles in segmenting the new market worth mentioning:

Guidelines for Segmentation

- To expose new opportunities, move beyond the obvious descriptors and find exciting ways to delineate different groups.
- Use descriptors which say why *segments* as opposed to *products* or services are different.
- Look not just in terms of who people are but also why, how, when, how often and for what they buy and use/could buy or use products and services.
- Don't stop at vertical industry segments – it's only a beginning.

There are several reasons for saying this.

First, industry segmentation won't get the new corporation closer to the end-user issues.

Second, you will find a lot of similarities which create potential segments which cut across industry verticals. (We don't even know how to define an industry anymore (more later).)

An example: banks and retailers, both being branch dependent, may be in different industries but they have similar needs for information technology (IT).

Or, given the similarities in the way they work, virtual sales teams or logistic operations from one industry, have similar needs to those in another industry – more so than they are similar to the accounting department in their own firm.

Seeing New
Segments First

It's worth reminding ourselves that those who "see" new market segments first will have a head start (provided they do something about it).

Underpinning Citibank's vision to be a global financial institution in the 1980s was the assumption that there was a group of mobile, wealthy customers who wanted the same services whether in Bangkok, Boston or Basle. (By 1993 the figure in Asia for Citibank customers had reached 45%!)

John Reed, the CEO, believes Citibank to be ahead in consumer global banking today because they moved more quickly than competitors into this segment (though competitors thought they were crazy at the time!).

He said:

"We made an important discovery that drove everything we did later . . . People's attitudes about their finances are a function of how they are raised, their education and their values, not just their nationalities. What works (for our market) in New York also works in Brussels, Hong Kong, and Tokyo. From day one therefore, we built the consumer business independent of geography."

Making
Market
Segment
Choices

Making dedicated choices about the markets in which companies want to excel goes beyond asking the usual questions, such as "what skills do we have to fit what market?"

Corporations ask:

* What market segments – existing, emerging *and* imagined – are out/could be out there?

And also:

* Which are likely to be the growth markets of the future?
* Are these accessible to us – how can we get in?
* What kind of competition is in there/likely to get in there?
* Where are we likely to be successful quickly, to demonstrate new capabilities?

How much time and effort goes into defining markets and segments very much depends on from whence an organization has come.

But let's be clear: the definition and choice of market(s) is not a tactical decision. It is a corporate decision integrally linked to the vision and fundamental to any

successful transformation aimed at customer "ownership".

As part of the education stage in the transformation
process, the more involvement in target segment(s)
choice by those who need to serve these customers, the
better. It is another way to move minds to markets and
get people who need to implement changes pulling in the
same direction.

CHAPTER 18

Moving Beyond Segmentation

While segmentation is an important step, it doesn't go far enough for new corporations driving to the market place.

Because no longer can firms produce one set of benefits for all members of a given market segment.

For example, within the banking segment, banks are different from each other in their IT needs, depending on their customers, culture and competitive philosophy.

Being (More) Things to Some People

Middle-agers would differ depending on why and where they wear jeans or their newly acquired body shape!

Transport and logistics, say, would require different things from packaging, depending on whether goods were large or small, perishable or not, high or low value.

Marketing managers needing IT solutions would have specific needs depending on, say, their route to market or sales setup.

Once segments are chosen, within them smaller clusters of user groups have to be identified who are *different* from others (see x axis of Figure 18.1), and this requires new corporations to customize part of their offering (see y axis) to serve these particular needs.

Going still a level further (see Figure 18.2) individuals and individual firms within these user groups (x axis) need a portion of the offering *individualized* especially for their *unique* needs and circumstances (y axis).

Being All Things to Some People

How much of the offering ends up being unique depends on the circumstances (though the figure shows equal sized squares).

The principle is this: for a part of the offering – either product or service, or both – exception becomes the rule.

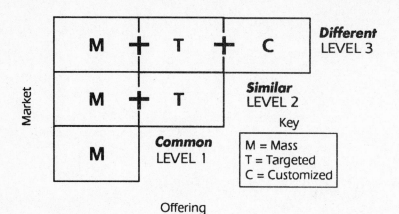

Figure 18.1   Reconfigurating the Market

Individualization doesn't mean adding a larger variety of products from which customers can now choose (an automobile manufacturer tried once to offer 87 different types of steering wheel hoping everyone would get something they liked – but the last thing customers wanted was to wade through a list of 87 steering wheels!).

Individualization is about getting products and services exactly right for those individual customers

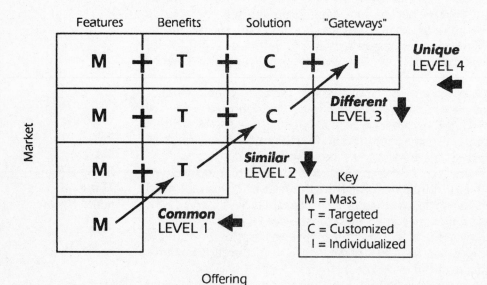

Figure 18.2   Reconfigurating the Market

within the target segment and user group with whom the corporation has decided to do business.

Which includes giving individuals different products and services at different times depending on the context and their differing role – in both their private or personal capacity.

"Variations" is a pool leasing scheme which enables car buyers (either individuals or their employers on their behalf) to drive any car they want when they want it (anything all of the time).

Mercedes and Porsche Pool Cars

For example, someone driving an executive Mercedes during the week may want another, more sporty car for weekends. One customer who drives one car during the summer drives another more appropriate vehicle for the winter. And the price for the year is adjusted to suit their individual menu of needs.

Instead of trying to get customers to own the car, the object is to give customers the kind of variety that they need to ensure the corporation can "own" them over time in a variety of differing circumstances.

"Mass customization" is a term being used in the literature to show how mass products can be made flexible enough to suit individual customers.

Going Part of the Way: Mass Customizing Levi Jeans

For instance, women have long pained over getting the correct fit of jeans to suit their own particular shape. Levi Strauss now customizes jeans in stores for women and, if all goes well, they intend to go ahead with the same formula for men.

The idea is that a sales assistant takes the measurements of a customer. The measurements are then entered into a computer which identifies the closest prototype (there are hundreds) to customize the fit.

Additionally, adjustments can be made by staff on a person's measurements and fed into the system. Three weeks later the customer receives the jeans for an extra $10.

Also in the fashion business is Bally, which now have the electronics to enable them to implement their mission of "total footware performance" for individual customers.

Will Bally Make Shoes for Individuals?

Measurements are taken of foot shapes (did you know that thanks to jogging, etc., the shape of feet has changed over the years in the Western world?) in order that new variations can be built into ranges for certain target groups. Millions of people have been measured worldwide, and Bally intends to do the next step and provide shoes fitted specifically for the foot shape and lifestyle of each customer.

In both cases the next step would be to personalize the entire customer experience instead of just the product, asking: how do individual customers want to buy jeans/ footware? Who are they? Do they want to come into a store in the first place? How do they want to pay? What happens when their jeans/footware are worn/washed/ repaired or need replacing?

Going Beyond Direct Marketing

Nestlé France segments the market for their branded goods in several ways for distribution through retailers, wholesalers and dispensing machines around the globe.

But through sophisticated technology they also are now able to follow the lives and development of customers and provide services which make products more usable according to their individual circumstance.

For instance when a child is born in France the name and details are recorded, so that mothers can phone in to get advice on nutrition – what products to use, when, how, and special diets based on the history and needs of that child's intake.

Ideally this goes beyond using technology simply for direct marketing.

Being in constant contact with individual customers, throughout their lives, the question is whether Nestlé and others will be able to produce individualized offerings for customers to cover their lifelong nutritional needs?

Ciba Geigy Individualizes Square Metres of Land

In a very different market, satellite technology (the same system which guided the missiles used in the Iraq war) can now customize soil per metre within a field so as to maximize a farmer customer's crops.

Whereas before farmers were spraying pesticides across the field according to Ciba Geigy's recommended *average* rate, now, depending on temperature, weather and other conditions, *individualized* solutions of mixtures and amounts can be self-mixed and applied to each square metre as needed.

(Note: Ciba could sell fewer chemicals in the process.)

Individualization: Tomorrow's Mass Market

Individualization of offerings is quickly becoming the route to tomorrow's mass market.

To commit customers to an ongoing lifetime relationship is to be able to individualize an offering especially for them.

Which means providing either all or part of the time (Refer to Figure 18.2):

- The *mass* based on *features* of the product or service – level 1.
- Plus the *benefits*, *targeted* to specific target segments – level 2.
- Adding to this a part of the offering, comprised of products and services, which is *customized* to provide *solutions* for specific user groups within segments – level 3.
- And, finally, adding to this whatever is needed to become an integrated *"gateway"* to a complete set of *individualized* customer solutions, over time, and their lifetime – level 4.

Individualization is increasingly feasible because information technology (IT) enables us to:

- Have continuous access to customers and they to us, making the relationships alive and ongoing.
- Interchange ideas and information in real time, and have interactive dialogue which gets and gives instant responses and feedback.
- Build institutional memory on customers, thus making offerings totally relevant for them in their own space.

The reconfiguration model is dynamic. Over time the mass or commodity part of the offering can be targeted, customized and individualized (see arrows on Figure 18.2).

And, similarly, the individualized portion of an offering – initially intended for a unique customer – can be transferred on to a wider group of customers thereby making products and services massified in order to gain economies (more in a later chapter).

Going back to the figure, try the following proposition on colleagues:

An Exercise on Market Re-configuration

- Individualization is tomorrow's mass market opportunity.

Then ask:

- At what level(s) are we currently operating?
- What do we have to do to move to individualization?

SECTION 7

MAKING COMMITMENT
ENDURING

We Have Met The Enemy And They Is Us.

Pogo – Cartoon Character

CHAPTER 19

Managing Resistance and Resistors

Iain Vallance, Chairman of British Telecom (BT), tells how difficult it was for the corporation to make the deep changes needed to become profoundly customer driven (on a global basis). This, despite the external pressures which many had assumed would be enough to bring about significant change.

What he says is that in retrospect he – like others – didn't realize the full measure of what was required and how radically it would have to be internalized to affect the old customs and systems operating at BT. Underestimated, he believes, was the resistance of the organization to be willing to change.

There is an important message in this. Despite everything that's said about what can be done to drive a corporation to the market place, managing resistance and resistors is a crucial part.

There are three "givens" in this respect.

One, resistance is not linked to seniority. Some of the most resistance you will find in the highest places.

Three Givens in Managing Resistance

Two, linked to this: often the most powerful people are those whose knowledge, feel and experience are most out of touch with new customer logic.

And, following this, three, the people who motivate and drive the corporation forward, and turn ideas, concepts and frameworks into a new corporate way, are to be found everywhere within the organization.

In an ideal world everyone would be thinking and feeling the same way at the same time, and we could just get on and do whatever needed doing.

Top management would definitely all be tuned in and turned on at the start, so that the change could move swiftly through the ranks from the articulation of a vision through to its implementation.

And every country would be on the same wavelength, responding in concert to customers' global and pan-European demands.

That change no longer moves hierarchically either "top-down" or "bottom-up" has been an important learning in the past decade. (In May 1994, at the height of the IBM crisis, the *Wall Street Journal* reported that some 20% of its top 1400 managers still hadn't accepted the fundamental need for change.)

"Pockets of resistance" need to be found and managed by change leaders.

Similarly, "pockets of support" need to be identified and given the direction and backing to do whatever is needed to make the right things happen at the right time to:

- Get the momentum going during the *agitation* phase.
- Then make new ways of working operational during the *education* phase.
- Institutionalize ways of behaving during the *integration* phase.

The theory on diffusion is quite simple. To escape barriers and delays sufficient numbers, i.e. a critical mass, of the correct people need to come together at the appropriate times to do specific things.

These people influence others by their behaviour and thereby bring about the transformation.

The Ciba Geigy Allcomm Experience

Taking internal services at Ciba Geigy and making them into independent profit centres was part of the radical transformation that took place in 1990 to transform the "lumbering supertanker", in the words of the chairman, "into faster, more manoeuvrable and market-driven ships".

Jurg Chresta was chosen to head one of these ships – the ex-internal advertising – which would become a new and fully independent unit which he would make into a leading European (then global) communications agency within two years.

Before, Ciba divisions and regions had no choice: they had to use the internal advertising (and other) head office services and they were allocated a cost accordingly. Now they could choose with whom to do business.

Chresta's challenge was to switch what amounted to a "civil service" mentality to one which would be competitive enough to excel in some of the fiercest markets in Europe.

Employees were not used to looking for business outside of Ciba – colleagues had been captive. How to shake off the old Ciba Geigy mindset in sufficient numbers of people was his biggest challenge.

Using Diffusion Theory

People – we know – take on new products at different rates. This diffusion process is also at work during a customer-driven transformation. More specifically:

- In the same way that people purchase new products at different rates so people buy into and take on new ideas and change their behaviour at different speeds.
- We can identify diffusion categories of people based on this notion, using them to motivate and manage the transformation process at the various different phases.
- Into what diffusion category people fit, depends largely on their "risk profile" – i.e. their willingness to switch behaviour without having certainty of the outcome.
- Into this "risk profile" is wrapped a whole lot of cultural and personal characteristics and preferences like previous experience, personality, fear, power drive, etc.
- The same logic can be applied to country organizations – by virtue of their culture, some will take on new ideas and concepts more quickly than others.

Those which are relatively authoritarian, still tend to be uncomfortable by the autonomy which characterizes transformations today – they often wait for others to move before they leap.

Reactions at Differing Speeds

Reaction to the profound changes needed in a customer transformation in mature corporations, at the peak of their performance (point 2 on the S curve – refer to S life cycle curve Chapter 3, page 11), will fall more or less into a "normal" distribution curve (Figure 19.1 illustrates).

Those corporations at point 1, more proactive by nature, will find the distribution of reactions skewed to the left, i.e. they will have more "innovators" and

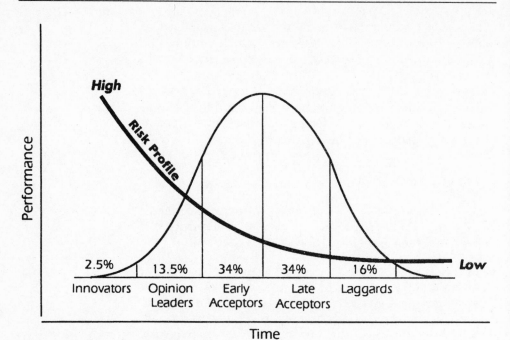

Figure 19.1   Diffusion Categories and Risk Profiles

"opinion leaders" – how much so will depend on circumstances.

A corporation in or near crisis – between points 2 and 3 – will find the distribution of reactions they get, tending to the right of the curve, i.e. they will have relatively more "early and/or late acceptors".

Profile of Diffusion Categories

Category 1

The "Innovators" (Shakers) (2.5% ±)

Of everyone, they have the highest risk profile and accept and enjoy change. From them the agitation comes. They are comfortable with innovation and uncertainty, sense competitive danger, work "from the guts", and pick up signals quickly – without requiring data as back up.

Impatient and intuitive – they "see" and sense market opportunities, projecting well into customer situations because they have a natural customer empathy, often based upon their own experiences.

They are the catalysts. Without them, nothing will happen or – if it does – it won't be the total shift needed to reach a new paradigm.

Innovators are both charismatic (they can influence) and credible (get people on their side).

They think longer term and are ultra-persistent, able, as one executive described it, "to run through walls to make what we believe must happen, happen".

They redefine the rules and boundaries as they go, and take others with them.

Typically they are curious: instead of looking at what's possible and making that happen, the innovator will aim for what most others consider impossible – and often try to make that happen.

Innovators can be very unpopular in traditional quarters – where "formal" power may still reside. If unmanaged, this can seriously hold up a transformation.

From the experiences of Jack Welch:

> ". . . so enthusiastic about his new strategy . . . so certain of its merit, that he [Welch] assumed his auditors would catch on at once. They did not. Welch grew increasingly frustrated. They had not caught on. They asked instead about how General Electric would do in the next quarter. They wanted numbers, not philosophy. . .
> . . . Welch was crushed. 'I knew I wasn't hitting a chord with them. My agenda and theirs were passing in the night.' He began yelling at them to relieve himself of some of the frustration. Nothing worked . . . How much had changed since then . . . In subsequent years . . . audiences digested every word of his philosophy and then went back to their offices and tried to put it into practice at once."

Once spotted and chosen as the change leader, the innovator needs to be buffered from the inevitable criticism.

This is especially important during the initial period when they have to get buy-ins from a small, powerful core group.

> "As Welch prepared to unhinge General Electric from its past, he benefited from having the board firmly in his corner. Walter Wriston, one of the most influential men in American business at the time and a GE board member since 1962, made a point of telling his acquaintances. 'We've got the greatest new CEO.' (Wriston reportedly did the same for John Reed when he first arrived at Citibank.)

Innovators enjoy being visible – both internally and externally communicating the vision, never tiring of or talking about customers' markets and the mission.

This is the kind of language they use:

"It just feels right."
"I'm going to stick with my feelings."
"The uncertainty is part of the fun."
"I don't know the details or how we are going to do it but I know it's right."
"I don't have the answers – you're the experts."
"It's obvious to me."
"Sounds right, do it."

Category 2

The "Opinion Leaders" (Movers) (13.5%)

This group has a high risk profile as well, and are essential to a transformation – a portion of this group buy in during the agitation phase (otherwise success is probably impossible).

Opinion leaders are the group that best help shape the vision and set a customer "ownership" agenda by getting key projects up and running.

They usually have reputation and strong relationships in the company.

When the education phase begins and the first initiatives are under way the size of the group quickly grows to 13.5%±.

The opinion leaders thus push the transformation forward. They become the focal point of customer efforts – the mouthpiece for, and advocates and sponsors of, the transformation.

They are to be found all over a corporation irrespective of seniority.

As trendsetters they influence people inside and out of the corporation (including customers).

They are the "missionaries", converting others as the transformation moves ahead, and similarly moving the transformation ahead as they convert and support those in the next diffusion category.

They are prepared to take risk, will experiment with new customer ideas, enjoying the challenge and excitement.

They easily take on a leadership role – and focus efforts and resources on customer priorities, accepting, spreading and using new language, concepts, frame-works, tools and ideas.

They are able to operate outside of the normal organizational procedures and structures, and do so to move the change along.

They use tangible results which can help influence others.

Typically here's how they talk:

"We need a new challenge."
"The way to do it is the way that works."
"Let's get something done."
"People can do things if you let them."
"Let's do it first and then get it perfect."
"We must learn to do the right things."

Category 3

The Early Followers (Wait-and-See-ers) (34% ±)

Conservative by nature and trade, they have a low(er) risk profile. They wait, sometimes resisting change until they understand better what's happening and what's working.

They may only feel a sense of urgency during the education phase of the process, when the first initiatives have already been started by some and the results are already being felt.

They thus take their lead from the opinion leaders – waiting, then committing.

Though at their worst they can block progress initially, they often counterbalance the opinion leaders, in terms of skills.

Exposure in specific projects builds confidence. Better at making new processes work and handling the operational issues, or issues that become operational, they are initially best used to manage the day-to-day activities.

When early acceptors begin to alter their behaviour, the transformation has really taken root. (Conversely, if they don't change their behaviour, the institutionaliza-tion of a new customer logic may never be accom-plished.)

Initially they say:

"Let's be sure before we jump."
"We need to do a better job of what we do well."
"You can't really delegate because people don't have the new skills."

"We need more experts."

"We've got the rules to obey."

"I don't know if we (I) have the skills."

"Tell us exactly what you want to do and we'll do it."

Category 4

The Late Acceptors (Blockers) (34% ±)

They are risk averse by nature. Found all over an organization, they buy in and participate only once the early acceptors have begun operating differently.

They are often happy with the *status quo*, continuing to rely on technical capability for success, not particularly seeing their role in the customer value adding process or the transformation.

At the beginning they say:

"We've tried this before and it failed."

"I don't see why we (I) have to change."

Sign of a breakthrough: they ask for more details.

Category 5

Laggards or *(Stoppers) (17% ±)*

They don't change. Some may want to leave – others usually have to go.

Diffusion Theory in Action

Back to Ciba Geigy Allcomm to illustrate diffusion in action.

Jurg Chresta went looking for and brought in three people from outside and combined them with three innovators from inside Allcomm to form what he called the "experimental group" (nicknamed the "chaos" group by others). These included a lawyer – who came from outside the advertising business – a talented artist, a secretary and a former communication unit misfit who had been looking for something new to do.

These new people were deliberately chosen because they were prepared to do whatever was necessary to become the new corporation, as articulated by the vision.

Chresta gave them the freedom to do this. "Show the world that you can get the business and satisfy the market. No one will interfere with you if you deliver the goods", he said. (Later on in the process he took the good and bad experiences learned from the "experimental group" and embedded these learnings and best practice into other departments.)

There was a group of younger "entrepreneurs" whom Chresta concentrated on initially, about 10% of the staff, who were very receptive, impatient to begin new projects and make their mark. They didn't care about the details and made the adjustments to find new and appeal to existing (Ciba Geigy) customers.

Another 30% were quite flexible and happy to get going once they saw what was going on and were able to do the kind of work they knew and liked and their status remained intact. Chresta gave them a different time frame, and a different set of customers to serve.

About 40% were resistant at first. They were afraid of taking decisions and making mistakes.

Chresta spent time with them, sharing successes and mistakes, once the transformation got under way, to spread a new, more enabling culture.

A small group, about 10%, was against the change. Another 10% left.

Chresta brought some new blood in as the old moved out – those with the fully fledged experience he needed plus young talent that he could mould.

But at the end of 1995, 60% of the original people were still there.

Chresta repeated the "experimental group" experience when, in 1995, he formed an international alliance with Young and Rubicom. He "borrowed" an executive from this large, global advertising agency to run the new international division at Allcomm; the executive was supported by a specially formed team so as to move the globalization projects on quickly.

What experience shows is that failing to manage the diffusion process can leave a corporation in transformation floundering.

To summarize, here are some key "do's' and "don'ts":

Some Key "Do's" and "Don'ts" on Using Diffusion

don't:
look for consensus initially
do:
find the opinion leaders and work through them, building a critical mass of influence, power and momentum

don't:
expect the whole top team to react or move at the same time or pace

do:

work with a few key players and build a strong coalition with whom, and through whom, you can work and grow understanding, commitment and sponsorship

don't:

choose people for important initiatives based on their former seniority

do:

go for high-impact individuals and teams – opinion leaders who will make the change happen by influencing others as they actively demonstrate new practices and successes

don't:

try to involve everyone at once

do:

find the "pockets" of individuals who are receptive and give them the resources, projects and support they need to succeed (more on this later)

CHAPTER 20

Using Diffusion to Get Commitment

Because people buy into customer-driven transformation at different speeds, not everyone will read the same signs the same way at the same time.

Some people will look at a situation and declare a crisis. Others will have the real thing staring them in the face and not see, sense or be able to articulate danger.

Some people will see a crisis only when the company is in danger of surviving – others see a crisis when there are opportunities that the corporation could miss out on.

Bringing diffusion into modern thinking means that change leaders must manage the paradoxes of letting things play out and, at the same time, influence to get the pace they want and need.

On New Year's Day 1990, Lars Kolind wrote a four page memo entitled "Thinking the Unthinkable" to try and get people in the Danish organization out of the lethargy that had persisted after the initial improvements made in the 1980s.

Oticon and "Thinking the Unthinkable"

Kolind had seen certain major competitors getting in first into the "lifelong hearing" market space, using the newest technologies which had moved hearing aids from behind to inside the ear.

But neither his concern for survival nor the opportunities Kolind sensed for the 1990s were shared inside the company:

> "I was really alone in wanting to take the company significantly further . . . Everybody including the board was saying we had really fantastic management. They were satisfied and wanted to leave things the way they were. I felt more alone than I had ever been."

Kolind deliberately used the memo as a triggering device and a way to get people swept up in the wave quickly, figuring out for themselves how to implement the change.

The memo stated his dream for the kind of company he wanted Oticon to be, leading in creativity and flexibility.

He asked all 150 employees to "think the unthinkable". Tossing out all assumptions about work and workplace, he challenged them to begin with a clean slate – all paper, all traditional jobs and walls would go to create a new customer-driven organization – they could decide how.

Lars had had enough discussions to know that the older, more traditional types were not only bewildered by his ideas but strongly opposed to them. Many of the younger people were receptive but many didn't really think it would materialize.

His decision to relocate to a remote part of Denmark caused outright resistance by everyone. Kolind retracted the decision and changed the location to an old brewery in Hellerup outside Copenhagen. Then he pushed for people to begin making changes in the way they worked, deliberately burning bridges to the past – including selling off all old furniture – to show that "they had reached the point of no return".

Like many others Oticon had to let people go as they discovered better ways of working.

But instead of firing the old-timers and keeping the younger, more aggressive ones, the company let those go who were best able to find jobs. To those who stayed Kolind announced (and then spoke to each personally) that they would have to support and contribute to the new company way.

Said Kolind:

> "It must have worked because they are all still here and we've done incredibly well. In retrospect I think they felt personally obliged – had they been inflexible and a blockage after that I would have fired them.
>
> But this doesn't mean you can just hope for the best. During the turbulent time in 1990 I picked people I knew were the drivers. I aimed for them and helped them find others.
>
> And five years down the line I still do it because we are still changing. But now they come to me with the ideas and I say "it sounds right; you go persuade the others – if you can, then go do it."

Accelerating "Time to Acceptance"

Corporations which want to "own" their customers have to begin to get commitment early on from the correct customers – managing diffusion externally as they must internally.

And, as is the case internally, some customers will react immediately – some will wait.

Before, with the emphasis on volumes, insufficient care went to choosing the correct customers at the very outset.

Accelerating "time to acceptance" by opinion leader customers will enable an organization to get to the bulk of their market.

Linear logic programmed corporations to get new products and services to market quickly so as to cover research and development (R&D) costs, penetrating the market fast to beat competition.

Today we make "innovator" and "opinion leader" customers part of the R&D and diffusion process.

Corporate customers become integral to the learning and credibility building needed to drive a corporation to the market place. They become partners, investing in making new ideas and frameworks operational.

Choosing Corporate Partners With Whom to Leap

Picking partners with whom to do projects so that the diffusion process works is, therefore, a critical success factor.

It entails finding and getting to the "innovator" and "opinion leader" organizations early on and/or "pockets" or persons within corporations who are influencers, leaders, or sponsors for a new way of working.

What category a corporation falls into (refer again to Figure 19.1 for diffusion categories) will clearly influence how quickly it is (or parts of it are) prepared to take on new ideas and working arrangements.

Remember, often the biggest (in revenue terms) customers won't be the first to accept or be the best bet in the long term.

The best choice for choosing partners initially are those corporations which will:

- Act as a reference source, both in product and experience terms.
- Give you entrée and an early start.
- Allow you to make a tangible difference to their business results.

- Invest time and money in making both the offering and the relationship work.
- Respect transparency and value sharing.
- Believe enough in the benefits to push within their firm, with and for you.

Changing the Economic Rules

Because these customer initiatives cannot pay off in the normal way or over the usual time horizons, how to get them funded is sometimes the biggest challenge.

To sort out are:

- How much time, energy and money are you prepared to invest to get the learning and know-how?
- How much of the exercise do you expect to be profit generating, and how much will go to make a worthwhile learning experience?
- How can you use the learning gained in a tangible way?
- How can you express this in the economics?
- What can you save if you get rid of working practices which cost money, but add no real end-user value (e.g. bidding)?
- Who does what, who pays for what, who gets what afterwards?
- How can you get the best people on both sides to make it work.

One way to finance initial customer commitment is to make them part of customer R&D. Most corporations have product R&D budgets so it is a practical way to get support and realistic return time frames agreed upon.

But trying to quantify gains is still important. Such as:

- What new product opportunities will come from this?
- What information and know-how can we extract?
- What is the potential worth of the information, know-how, learning, confidence and credibility we will gain?

SECTION 8

JUMPING INTO THE CUSTOMER'S ACTIVITY CYCLE

To see the World in a grain of sand
And A Heaven in a wild flower
Hold Infinity in the palm of your hand
And Eternity in an hour

William Blake

CHAPTER 21

You Know You "Own" the Customer If . . .

You are their first choice.

They look to you to solve their problems.

They share confidential information with you.

They talk to you about their plans.

They accept your advice and ideas.

You are involved early on in their decisions.

They discuss options (as opposed to just price and discounts) with you.

They give you feedback (good or bad) before you ask.

They recommend others to you (and you to others).

They trust you to take decisions on their behalf.

They want you to succeed.

CHAPTER 22

The Value Add is in the Experience

If you've ever been exposed to Tao wisdom you'll know that it is a Chinese philosophy based on the totality of the experience.

The most simple translation of Tao (pronounced Dow) is the "way", the "path" or the "journey". The ancient mystics in China expressed it as the "way" of the cosmos, the "way" of the universe, the "way" of nature, the "way" of man.

The main point they made was that each point in a journey or "way" was interrelated and interdependent, so forming one ongoing flow.

To miss one part was to disrupt this flow – to consider each small part on its own, in isolation, was to miss the overall effect.

No matter what product or service we are talking about, customers respond holistically:

Following the Customer's Experience

We may see different products, services companies or industries.

They see a flow which delivers (or doesn't deliver) the result they are after.

We may be producing a whole lot of diverse inputs – bits and pieces in our corporate or individual chains and channels. But *they* see (or don't see) a delivered output – in one integrated space.

Failure to understand and make operational the distinction make us vulnerable.

A remark by Stan Davis – world guru on business strategy – makes the point:

"When an airline loses a customer's reservation . . . the
customer does not respond mechanistically and say, 'it is
only this one small part of the whole that is not good'.
The customer . . . (says) 'you don't know how to run an
airline' . . . the entire airline is on line in that one
moment."

The notion of becoming a "gateway" takes the new
corporation yet a step further.

When a plane's wheels touch down "on time" but the
customer is subjected to various delays and queues from
waiting for the door to open, stairs, buses, and baggage
to arrive to finding a cab to get them from the airport to
their destination they thus arrive stressed, tired and late.
And when this happens often enough to enough
customers, the whole airline/travel industry in on the
line.

The Carpet
Buying
Experience

The point is that if the flow in the experience breaks
down at end-customer level everyone suffers.

Many end-users' householders, DuPont found, had
intended to buy new carpeting during the prior 12
months, but had postponed doing so because going
through the total experience was so much of an ordeal.

The problem started because they felt insecure as to
where to go for what. Once inside a store, the situation
became even more confusing. Stores were depressing and
service bad. They had difficulty visualizing the carpets in
their home and didn't trust the salespeople – finding
them unsympathetic, uninformed and motivated only to
close a deal.

The ordeal did not end there. Deliveries were
unreliable and fitting was a nightmare. After having
been fitted, retaining the appearance of the carpet was a
constant worry and spills caused stains – repair, billing
enquiries, and several other aspects of their relationship
with retailers added to the frustrations.

Customers, DuPont realized, wanted a "gateway" to
floor covering solutions over a lifetime. It would take the
lead in providing the value add services needed to make
this happen.

Cross-unit teams for the commercial market were
formed, consisting of decoration, technical design and
maintenance people. They would help the various
institutions, stores and industries that used carpeting on
their floors or in their products (e.g. cars) make better
decisions. As well as get superior fitting and maintenance
and replacement.

These teams consisted of both insiders and outsiders brought together as needed for specific projects.

As far as the residential market was concerned, there would no more be a salesperson in the traditional sense of the word. Rather, a marketing person, a merchandizer and a technical person from DuPont would work together in teams, specially assigned to customers to make sure end-users got total results.

Accepting and fixing the mismatch between how people act and react holistically as customers and how units/countries/corporations have organized and behaved in the past is central to the customer transformation challenge.

The Tao of Citibanking

Research had shown that most people considered banking, for example, to be a disjointed experience, full of time-consuming activities, yet lacking in those they really needed.

It was in the early 1990s when Citibank embarked on their "Citibanking" mission – a new approach to doing business with customers, which heralded the next leap in the life of the financial institution.

For Citibank the object was to give customers an ongoing global experience, whether they were in a branch or in their car, in the high streets, at home or in their office – from Munich to New York or Tokyo.

Although management had positioned Citibank as *the* global bank, in the 1980s deregulation and technological advances had made conventional ways of dealing with customers redundant. In the past, being global had meant "being in several countries". But typically, local customers had had to scramble to manage and coordinate their financial affairs cross-border themselves.

Came the 1990s and increasing numbers of well-to-do geographically mobile customers demanded an integrated and consistent offering (whatever, wherever, whenever).

The quest in the consumer banking division was to try to get a common global idea of the various parts of the customer's banking experience, so that then, the various parts of the institution could be aligned to these activities.

As top management saw it, the customer's experience began when an account was opened, continued as customers used the facilities to manage their financial affairs on a daily basis, and was extended either locally or in other countries when the customer moved around or expanded their financial dealings.

This all had to be embraced into one cohesive global offering taking into account the needs of the individual within customers.

CHAPTER 23

The Customer Activity Cycle (CAC) Tool

By understanding the results customers are after, and mapping the critical activities in their experience that go to achieve these results, new corporations are able to identify the potential for *adding* value.

The customer activity cycle (CAC) is a methodology which enables these new corporations to do this in a creative yet practical way.

The CAC is not a model of buying behaviour. Rather it encompasses the whole set of activities a customer goes through pre, during and post experiences to obtain a result.

Generally speaking experiences span three distinct stages:

Pre
When the customer is *deciding what to do.*

During
When the customer is *doing it.*

Post
When the customer is *keeping it going and updating it.*

While the stages clearly overlap, the intervals provide a convenient generic framework for analysis and exploration (see Figure 23.1).

The method applies quite generally across the board, to almost any situation ranging from an eating experience in a restaurant, or buying footware, to setting up a global banking networking capability, or building a new automobile factory.

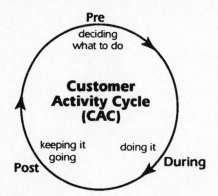

Figure 23.1   The Customer Activity Cycle (CAC) Tool

Starting Point for Creating Value

The methodology hence provides a general framework for a corporation switching from the traditional sequential model of yesteryear, to one which begins with end-users.

All decisions internally, within the new corporation, and externally, within the supply/distribution channel, begin with end-users and their activity cycles and then work back (see Figures 23.2 and 23.3).

Everything worth doing is destined to discovering and delivering added value to end-users.

The Customer Activity Cycle (CAC) as a Transformation Tool

The CAC methodology serves different purposes at each phase of a transformation process.

At the start – at any and all levels – it acts as an *agitation* device and effective trigger for radical change. People see the difference between what they have been good at doing and what is now needed.

As an *educational* tool, it forces people into the customer's space and provides a common view and tool to see what customer value really means, and what it would take to *add* to this.

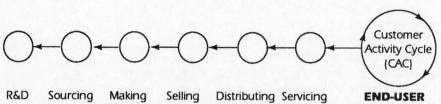

R&D   Sourcing   Making   Selling   Distributing   Servicing   **END-USER**

Figure 23.2   The CAC as the Starting Point for Creating Value Internally

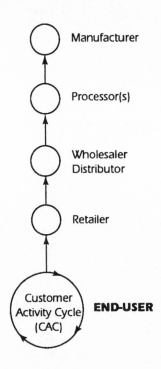

Figure 23.3   The CAC as the Starting Point for Creating Value Externally

Everyone involved in building the new corporation is pointed in the same direction – at the critical value adding opportunities on the customer activity cycle.

With the methodology in place, new customer logic, therefore, becomes *actionable*. The efforts of individuals/units/countries/companies begin to converge around a single organizing principle.

Used across the business(es) it becomes the *integrative* mechanism.   People/units/countries/companies   see either how they fit (or don't fit) into a new framework – dealing either with external and/or internal customers.

New corporations acknowledge that to add value they need to know what customers *do (will do)* not just who they *are*.

Recalling a quote used in a previous chapter by David Whitwam of Whirlpool:

Managing the Customer's Value Adding Process

"... the hard part ... is when you take your clothes out of
the dryer and have to do something with them – iron,
fold, hang them up. Whoever comes up with a product to
make this part of the process easier, simpler or quicker is
going to create an incredible market."

New corporations accept as well that:

Real value happens only in the *customer's space.*

In *their space* they only accumulate *costs.*

Let's go back to Northumbrian Water.
They had been taking fresh water to, and collecting the
dirty from, various corporate customers for decades.
But as one director put it:

"We realized we needed to get 'behind the factory gate' if
we were going to deliver real value add to customers.

Industrial customers are very reliant on water for the
quality of their products – the taste of everything you eat
and drink is affected by water as is the consistency of that
taste from day to day or country to country. The drugs
you use could contain as much as 90% water. The quality
of the microchips in PCs depend on water.

But some of our largest water-using industrial clients
were taking their water (conforming you'll recall to 99.8%
industry standards) and putting it into tanks marked
'raw ingredient'.

Only then did the real value adding begin."

Discovering Opportunities Through the Customer Activity Cycle (CAC) Methodology

The first step in any CAC exercise is to map the critical
value adding points customers go through to get the
results they want. (These customer results should
coincide with the corporation's mission such as "trouble-free operations", "networking capabilities", "document management", etc.)

Next, follows an assessment of the opportunities for
adding value at each of the critical points which lead to
the results sought.

Let's look at some cases covering a range of industries
(figures are simplified).

Case 1: IBM   The IBM case demonstrates the customer activity cycle
for a corporate customer (say a bank) in the IT
"networking capability" "market space".

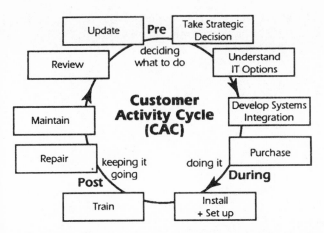

Figure 23.4   Customer Activity Cycle: IBM Bank Customer (Simplified)

Next is a customer activity cycle for "total footware performance" showing a "primary cycle" *plus* a "dependent cycle", which is a more detailed activity cycle of one of the primary points – in this case customer(s) "go(es) to store".

Case 2: Bally Shoes

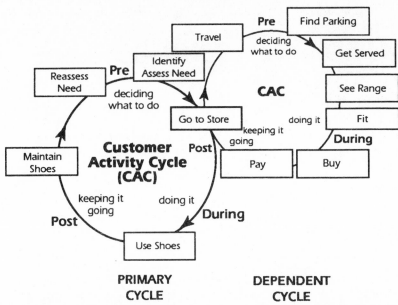

Figure 23.5   Primary and Dependent Customer Activity Cycles: Bally Customer (Simplified)

Case 3:   The next customer activity cycle is for the upmarket
Citibank   global Citibank customer segment, within the financial
                 services "market space".

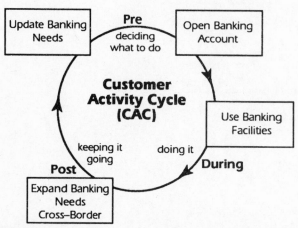

Figure 23.6   Customer Activity Cycle: Citibank Global Customer (Simplified)

Now we look at some of the value adds Citibank has
developed at each of these critical points.

With "on-line" relationship opening, the banker asks
the customer all the relevant information. This is
immediately entered into the computer, so creating a
master document which can be continuously updated.

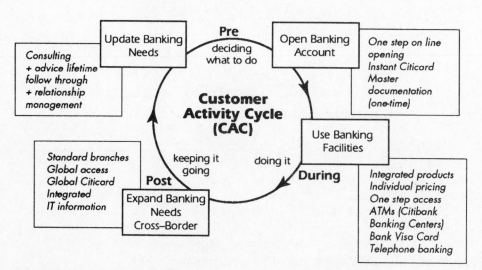

Figure 23.7   Value Adds on Customer Activity Cycle: Citibank (Simplified)

The initial customer questioning process should never have to be repeated.

Phones are automatically diverted during the interview, and workstations are equipped with printers, etc., so that forms can be produced there and then. The Citibank card, with the customer's name and number, is also created on the spot.

From home, customers can use their phones to make banking transactions and get information, including paying bills in some countries, obtaining a balance, requesting loans, making transfers and obtaining a cash slip for use in certain stores to purchase goods.

Calls are handled day or night. When customers go into the branch they can use their Citicard to get into an electronic queueing device, and so make a request in advance to save time.

The Citi-statement consolidates all transactions and pricing is individualized depending on the customer's overall portfolio.

Telephone service link-ups enable customers to manage their accounts around the clock and globe in several currencies.

The Citicard is intended to give customers access to almost any branch. With it, they get their European/worldwide balance in their own currency and all of their usual services. Following through on the relationships requires consulting and ongoing advice on lifetime investments and financial decisions. Superior investment prowess and results for customers, Citibank finds, is where customers are making increasing demands.

"Value Gaps" as Black Holes

What happens when a corporation or industry doesn't provide the added value at critical points in the customer activity cycle?

Discontinuities or disconnects – interruptions in the flow – cause "value gaps", creating "black holes" which:

- Destroy or weaken the chances of customers getting the results they want, both in the overall experience, and from individual products and/or services.
- And, importantly, these "black holes" open up opportunities for others (most often from outside traditional industry definitions) to get into the cycle and establish a relationship at key points.

I have my own version as to why IBM lost customer
"ownership" in the 1980s and early 1990s.

The same principles can be applied to almost all
business situations.

A focus on *product* rather than *customer process*
inhibited the development in services, skills and partnering needed to give the customer a desired experience and
result.

This led to "value gaps" in the customer's activity
cycle (as Figure 23.8 shows), opening up just the
opportunities others needed to get into a relationship at
critical times.

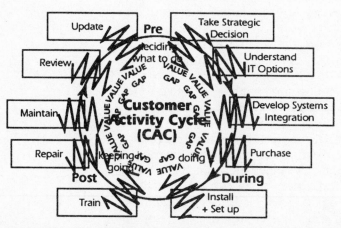

Figure 23.8   "Value Gaps" in the Customer Activity Cycle: IBM Customer (Simplified)

By the time a consulting company had been with a
corporate customer for months, participating in and
analysing their strategy, and/or a software firm had been
working on a customer's systems, the best IBM could
hope for was to win on price and specification.

Maintenance and repair (though earning millions)
were still considered mundane then. The "dungarees
and spanner brigade" is how one executive described it.

These post services, routine and reactive, had become
indifferent to customers, and as a commodity enabled
third party operators "lean, keen and mean" to fill that
value gap.

Without a relationship base to review and update
decisions, staying in the customer activity cycle, so as to
sustain relationships, became increasingly difficult.

The following case is not about IBM, but it comes from the same industry.

A manufacturer ordered two sets of 20 PCs from their local VAR (value added retailer).

Here's how the IT manager explained her experience:

"The machines finally arrived. One person (subcontracted?) did the delivery – the boxes were left in reception.

I had to get people to help me get the boxes to the offices, where two of us spent two weeks unpacking, getting rid of old machines, storing and taking away the packaging and old manuals – for which an entire office had to be cleared – and getting everyone trained up and running."

As these examples demonstrate "value gaps" are often more about what corporations *don't do* (or do, but don't get the customer to see the value of doing) rather than what they do badly.

Through "value gaps", customer "ownership" easily swings to newcomers who, as they become closer to customers and are able to personalize offerings and cement long-term relationships, increasingly take over the lucrative opportunities.

Needless to say some couriers, transportation companies and others have seen the long-term value of customers, hence they have closed the gap. Now they buy, warehouse, deliver, unpack, install, etc., PCs, as well as other office equipment, taking back the unwanted packaging, machinery, etc.

Much of the new IBM effort is to fill these "value gaps" as Figure 23.9 shows:

Time to Talk About a New IBM

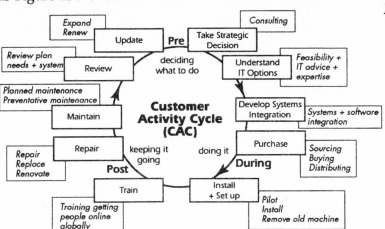

Figure 23.9 Value Adds in the Customer Activity Cycle: IBM (Simplified)

Looking clockwise, from the top of the activity cycle in Figure 23.9, corporate customers (say a bank) start by figuring out where they are going strategically and what they need to do (can do) with IT to get the value added to their end-users, and consequently to those people/machines in the bank to become the successful servers. For this they need consulting.

They then need the software and data management systems, which enable people/machines to interact and perform with and for their customers in an integrated way.

Then, and only then, do customers look for the technologies (the T in the IT) available, and source, buy and connect the pieces that go to make the ultimate value add solutions.

Machines need to be installed, people trained (a huge proportion of downtime is still due to the business system and people rather than the equipment), and old machines and packaging disposed.

Customers need ongoing use of the machines, planned preventative and remote repair, and maintenance to avoid any undue interruptions – whatever the reason. And, when and where failure does occur, they need immediate recovery help, without having to hop from one supplier or part of the organization to another.

After review – an activity which should be ongoing – customers need to be able to expand and develop their system through constant renewal, based on the planning and flexibility that went into the initial decisions.

An Example of "Primary" "Dependent and "Sub-Cycles"

A customer activity cycle exercise starts with a "primary cycle".

This needs to be exploded to form the "dependent cycles" as the Bally example and Figure 23.5 have demonstrated.

Figure 23.10 goes deeper into one point on a "**primary cycle**" – "update" – for an IBM UK services banking customer division, which manages the cash dispensing and other non-branch financial services the bank offers to end-users.

IBM, having done a customer activity cycle with the bank to see what value their customers (end-users) go/could go through, to get the value add delivered at each critical point in a cash (or other non-branch financial services) experience, now asks:

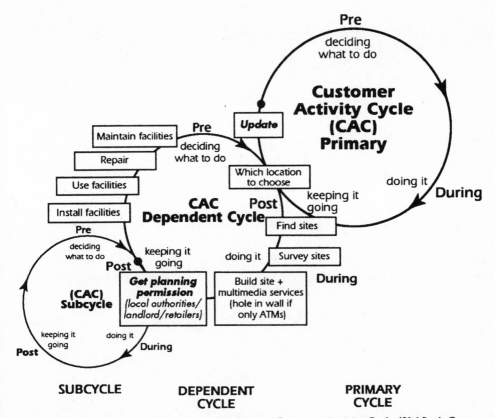

Figure 23.10 Dependent and Subcycle on the Primary Customer Activity Cycle: IBM Bank Customer

1. What would the critical value add points on the bank's activity cycle be so that they could deliver the needed value adds at each of the end-user critical points?

Then, taking one point – "update" in this case – a more detailed "**dependent cycle**" is done, asking the next question:

2. What is the role of IT in achieving the critical value adds during the "update" cycle of the kiosk network?

Then:

3. How can we as IBM translate this into new and improved products, services and solutions?

To recap:

End-users – persons wanting speedy, secure, non-branch cash (and other finance services), going through a series of activities to achieve this, as part of their total financial service needs.

Customer – part of the bank, building and managing ATMs and ATM kiosks for end-user market segments.

Value adding point to look at in more detail – the "update" ATM kiosk network activity, creating a "dependent cycle".

The figure also goes a step further showing a "**subcycle**" at one critical point; namely "get planning permission" on the "update" dependent activity cycle.

Ground Rules for Using the Customer Activity Cycle Technology

Here are some ground rules for using the customer activity cycle (CAC):

1. Start with end-users and work backwards to see what will lead to the their desired results.
2. Ask what customers do/could do through their activity cycle, at each critical point in their experience to get these results – look at the total picture.
3. When identifying opportunities don't get side-tracked by what you presently do – think about current opportunities but also about those in the future.
4. Concentrate on finding product and service opportunities that ensure getting into the CAC sooner and staying in longer.
5. Find a point of entry, working from strength but simultaneously seek to build credibility and confidence in other parts of the CAC.
6. Include people interfacing with the customer and implementing strategies in CAC "workshopping".
7. Involve customers in CAC workshops – it's a way to get interactive research, learning and commitment.
8. Allow people to think freely and creatively about possibilities – but keep on track by going back to the vision, stated mission and "market space".
9. Use judgement in deciding on the amount of detail you need.
10. Try to verify what you have done with colleagues and customers but don't try and "prove" anything – there is no right answer.

SECTION 9

GETTING INTO THE CUSTOMER'S HIGH GROUND

You Cannot Step Twice into the Same River

Heraclitus

CHAPTER 24

Putting Value In *and* Taking Non-Value Out

Being neutral – because it focuses on end-users – the CAC is an effective engaging tool, during the agitation and education phases of a transformation process.

People from different organizations, or different parts of a business or channel, focus on how to get value downstream and this becomes a powerful binding mechanism.

Involvement of the relevant people in the customer activity cycle exercises is essential. Then much can be achieved, not least of which is dialogue and discussion, from which a common picture and implementation plan begins to emerge.

From this, in turn, comes a commitment to joint projects which move the transformation visibly and tangibly forward.

High Value at Low Delivered Cost

There are two ways the new corporation adds value at the critical points identified in the CAC.

One, they *put value in* by providing products, services and solutions which:

- lead to a better result
- save time, hassles and/or money, improving the customer's experience along the way
- fill existing "black holes" – the discontinuities or disconnects in the CAC
- help customers do something themselves

- do for customers better/cheaper what they presently do themselves

Two, they *take non-value out* by:

- eliminating activities absorbing time, energy and money which don't add value to end-users
- eliminating activities being duplicated by themselves, customers and/or partners

With modern customers ever more demanding, unwilling to pay for waste or unnecessary overheads, new corporations must become a high value provider at low delivered cost.

The principle is simple:

- Everything that's necessary to be done, to get the value to customers on their activity cycle, gets done by the corporation or its partners.
- Everything that doesn't add this value gets eliminated.

Zurich Insurance Canada

As part of its transformation, Zurich Insurance – which hitherto had solicited several quotes from diverse subcontractors before agreeing to a job to fix a damaged home – decided to use one subcontractor per area in Canada.

Now, a subcontractor is committed (previously they cut prices to get the deal); they are on site immediately (given funds in advance if needed); finish the job much more quickly (saving total expenses); and customers are better off and say so, not having had to live in a hotel for long periods of time.

Huge expenses have been saved by Zurich Insurance – all the activities that went into finding the subcontractors, deciding whom to use, etc. People who were in a administrative position, filling filing cabinets, are now on the front line interacting with customers, making sure the job is done on time.

Baxter Health Care USA

Similarily, Baxter Health Care USA have built a system whereby value is added while non-value is taken out, this time in the health management arena, to accelerate comfort and healing for end-user patients.

Baxter deals with large hospitals, and whereas before all effort was on R&D that went into machines, it's now centred on providing expertise to give pre-diagnostics during the pre-operative/stay stage of the customer activity cycle, as well as special drugs administered directly to speed up the patient's recovery; and support to make the various activities during the operative/stay stage more efficient and effective (from the provision of special surgical gloves to help with supporting the patient, and assisting in the administration and managing of staff).

At the post-operative/stay stage, recently discharged patients get home-care help, 24 hour emergency advice, on-call nursing and transportation to and from the hospital.

All of this is done at a fraction of the cost of staying in the hospital.

Costly activities – like premixing drugs for individual patients, keeping stock and updating limited shelf-life drugs, and quality checking – are also performed for the hospital to get the non-value out of the system.

Baxter uses its size and expertise to do things more cheaply and avoid duplications between the various suppliers, thereby freeing up hospital resources to concentrate on patient care and rehabilitation, to firmly entrench relationships with doctors, patients and their families.

"Post Its" are useful in doing a customer activity cycle exercise.

Using "Post Its"

On a flip chart during brainstorming and planning sessions, get people to identify the customer activity cycle and use different colour "Post Its" – one colour for the customer's value adding points; another to identify the opportunities for putting value in, and a third colour for taking the non-value out.

Here is a random illustration from a workshop:

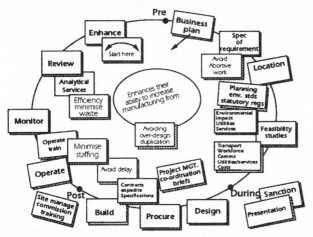

Figure 24.1   Illustration of Post Its in a CAC Exercise

CHAPTER 25

Changing the Nature of
the Customer Relationship

Once we start talking about the individualization of
offerings and becoming a "gateway" to a set of solutions
for customers, we need to figure out how to get into their
high ground – where the action and opportunities for
influence, revenue and commitment really are today.

It is in this high ground where customers review, take
and retake decisions on direction, and link operational
decisions to the improvement and protection of their
professional and personal lives.

It is also, however, at these stages in the CAC – usually
pre and post – where most of the "value gaps" have
occurred in the past.

Market making missions can only be implemented
with relationships solidly in the high ground. Getting
there is a corporate rather than a sales challenge – an
essential part of becoming profoundly customer driven.

The "Bowtie"
Blockage

The object is to build capabilities within the firm which
enable people to get through the "mahogany doors" into
the management corridors and boardrooms; and through
the "garden gate" – so to speak – into customers' homes
and longer-term aspirations and plans.

But when people are asked to actually go out and form
these deep new customer relationships, they inevitably
find that some of their organization's best contacts are
with people who don't necessarily understand, know or
care about the deeper more strategic implications of their
products and services.

Typically in corporations, traditional buyers have
made the choices as to with whom to do business.

Many have regarded many products and services – other than the major investments – as low interest or commodity items, which they could obtain anywhere.

Not having always looked at the value add possibilities, nor the total effect of these products and services on users, and often, not having figured out the total integrated cost of operating successfully, buyers have frequently made bad decisions which have not led to value for either users, or their end-customers.

The "bowtie" blockage is a term attributed to Procter and Gamble depicting the one-on-one relationship which prevailed between buyers and sellers in the 1960s, 1970s and 1980s (see Figure 25.1).

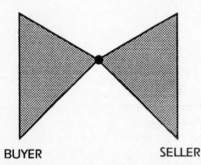

BUYER   SELLER
Figure 25.1   The "Bowtie" Blockage: Unilateral Corporate Customer Relationships

This, more often than not, was the main connection between the firm and its customers (unless things went wrong).

The "space" where the two sides of the "bowtie" meet – i.e. buyer and seller interaction – was narrowly defined, unilateral and confining, and often based on the lowest possible denominator – price.

And the opportunity for value add, collaboration and commitment was hence very limited.

Forging Multiple Customer Relationships

The move from making and moving products to providing value during a customer's total process requires a shift in the relationship between corporations and their customers.

From a past based on unilateral connections between corporates, which led to "high volume" buying and selling, the future will depend on building relationships

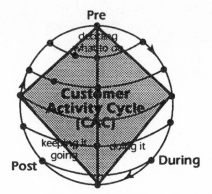

Figure 25.2 Multiple Corporate Customer Relationships

with several different customer groups and individuals, at various levels.

Looking at this visually in Figure 25.2, above the "bowtie" becomes a set of interactive connections between counterpoints, at each critical point on the CAC.

Increasingly, customers will be looking for single source (or fewer) suppliers as partners, so as to free themselves to spend time, energy and resources on their own extended core activities.

Making "Gatekeepers" Into "Door-openers"

Rather than the sellers providing bits and pieces which buyers then must put together and make work, customers are moving towards "one contact – one contract" relationships, involving deeper and longer-term commitments on both sides.

Pressured by their organizations to become value adders (instead of goods providers), the role of the traditional buyer within corporations is changing. They are becomming advice givers, problem solvers, relationship builders, integrators.

Before, they were trained to look at specification and price – and were judged accordingly.

Now they are evolving into "gateways" within their own corporations, supplying the sets of solutions (rather than the items) to their internal customers at critical delivery points in *their* activity cycles.

Their changing role from buyers, i.e. "gatekeepers" to "dooropeners", means they become facilitators and key contact points, encouraging dialogue and interaction with product and service providers at multiple levels within their organizations.

**Rank Xerox
and the
Taxman**

The shift in mentality from "gatekeeper" to "gateway" – from making and taking financial decisions to producing sets of solutions – requires a radical change in the behaviour of both buyers and sellers.

Both need to know and serve "benefit holders" instead of just "budget holders".

Both need to know who these benefit holders are.

Finding out is the first step. Rank Xerox had been dealing with professional buyers in local governments for decades. When it made its move to become the "document management" company, its management had to go and find out who it was within these institutions who could benefit most.

What they found in local UK government departments, for example, was that it was the group responsible for collecting the taxes, producing the tax bills and collecting the money who most needed help on better documents.

The tax bill was probably the only communication they had with customers, and the better formulated and looking the document, Rank Xerox postulated, the more they could increase the response rate of tax payment, thereby decreasing their costs.

Also, a better looking and functioning document would improve the local government's image among taxpayers. (Both these points proved true.)

**Defining the
High Ground
Relationship**

To develop the high ground relationships with customers we must – as mentioned in the previous chapter – work by the principle that we want to get into the customer activity cycle sooner, and stay in longer.

That way we can influence as well as anticipate what is to come, building that knowledge into our offering and resources planning.

If the object is customer value, being present and influencing at the pre stage of the CAC must be good for both parties, as is being present post use/delivery/ project/experience or whatever, when customers are reviewing and updating their decisions and going into the next loop.

One of the exercises done by Jiffy Packaging was to look at motor industry customers so as to reduce the considerable amount of damage to spare parts in transit. (Did you know that around 45% of the body panels manufactured in the UK arrive at their destination damaged!)

What they realized, however, was that the real opportunity for value adding began right at the outset with the design of the new auto model and the various components which go to make up the vehicle – during production and then as spare parts during maintenance.

Any packaging and transportation solution that could cut damage and so reduce costs would need involvement early on and throughout the entire process of designing, making, distributing and handling.

In a high ground relationship between corporations, providers and receivers commit to jointly develop a customer focus, aimed at getting value downstream.

Involvement needs to be at a strategic level, with the visible commitment of senior management on both sides – starting with board members.

Each firm has respective roles which are achieved through dialogue, workshopping and joint projects.

This is different from talking about partnering, but actually practising supply management.

- In the latter each party tries to get the best deal.
- In the former win/win situations are actively created by all – both parties are prepared to give something up to achieve common goals.
- In the latter the details determine the deal.
- In the former the deal comes first – the details are worked out.

Understandably in the initial stages of a transformation firms don't want the high level initiatives to interfere with routine sales and relationships.

The trick is to manage the routine and high ground activities concurrently, gradually integrating them in an organized and transparent way.

Getting in sooner, staying in longer and connecting at multiple levels require a different level of commitment on both sides – trust, transparency and a sharing of goals and information.

Finding a Point of Entry

This challenge is over and above the very practical need to find or create a suitable and immediate point of entry on the CAC from which a credibility and confidence base can be built.

Finding a point of entry involves figuring out where to spend time and whom to talk to.

Which means knowing:

- Where decisions are made and who influences whom.
- What the contact points are through the customer activity cycle that need managing and at which levels.

- Matching the correct people with their counterpoint customers.

An important question is whether the various customers involved in the total relationship differ in terms of their needs and priorities.

And the answer is that often not only may they want different things, their needs and expectations may be at odds with each other.

Baxter Health Care USA Builds Multiple Relationships

The principle in multiple relationships is that presence and contact is maximized rather than minimized at each critical point in the CAC.

And that rather than being a cost, the time, energy and resources spent at the various levels of interaction are part of the new corporation's investment portfolio.

(There is one proviso: presence and contact must add value – either directly or indirectly, either in the short or longer term.)

A for instance: Baxter Health Care has its warehouse workers team up with those working in the warehouses at the hospitals.

Designated people serve specific customers and two or three times a month they will jump on the delivery truck and ride it to that customer, to talk and look at ways to continuously add value to customer's activities such as unloading, unpacking and getting products where they need to go.

Similarly the accounts receivable people have built contact with their accounts receivable counterparts and their finance people with the customer's finance people, etc.

One of their senior managers expanded:

"They [these contacts] bind the customer to us and made it difficult for anyone who may try to take the business away. What we have found is that these non-sales relationships which are focussed on issues that are relevant to the customer are among the strongest selling features that we have."

British Telecom's "Calling Executive Programme"

British Telecom have taken their top 70 executives (including the chairman), and, based on their interests, knowledge and experience, each takes on a, or a series of, "calling executive" roles with select customers.

Contact for these calling executives ranges from boardrooms through IT management to users. This is part of the BT transformation to "own" customers and individualize offerings.

Calling executives also work with the customer teams including sales, services and support and help with the solution building, sales negotiations and troubleshooting within BT to ensure contact management at each critical point in the activity cycle.

Two challenges have been paramount in this effort:

- Getting commitment from top managers, needing a reprioritization of time and effort.
- Defining the respective roles of the various contributors at each point of customer contact.

Learning to Wear Multiple Hats

In new corporations, people learn to wear several hats, having to do several things simultaneously.

At certain times in the transformation, they will have to handle new initiatives and projects in addition to conducting "business as usual".

Efficiencies must be gained by getting rid of non-value add workloads and activities, to reinvest in building dedicated customer know-how and relationships.

Having more intense and multiple relationships with customers mean redeploying people into key customer contact positions and reskilling and retooling them.

They may have to make decisions for their local area, as well as for the company as a whole.

Or for their division, while also and, concurrently, for the entire organization.

They become the customer ambassador, in addition to an operator of the company.

They may have to develop a line of business or a target segment, while also manage a customer, or set of customer accounts.

People will find themselves competing and collaborating with colleagues, competitors, suppliers and customers simultaneously.

And deal with different customers who on some occasions compete, while on others collaborate.

Before, it was enough to *differentiate the corporation* through products and services.

Now corporations need to provide products and services to *differentiate the customers*.

Given new challenges, new corporations must replace the old notion of "job descriptions", which stated what tasks a person performed, with "skills descriptions", in which what people know becomes the crux (more later on).

Also they need to reward people (and teams) differently and reward different people and teams for doing different things at different times during the transformation.

SECTION 10

BUILDING NEW "COMPETITIVE SPACES"

A poem should not mean but be.

Archibald Macleish

CHAPTER 26

In Search of New Building Blocks

So far we've discussed what and where to add value in a new corporation.

Next comes by whom and how to organize.

For dealing with what turns out to be quite a complex part of the transformation, let's relook at some fundamentals on organizing.

Relooking the New Fundamentals

What we've said or implied so far is that:

1. Old linear and sequential value chains are no longer the building blocks for competitiveness – we need an alternative model or representation with which to work.
2. Customers couldn't care less how we are structured, who owns or reports to whom, so long as they get the results they want – delivered when, where and how they want them.
3. A lot of what corporations have been doing and on which they have been spending time, money and energy has had to do with perpetuating verticalized organization forms, in which people have been kept separate.

This has hampered the corporate customer relationship.

4. While this seems an obvious enough statement, taken into the higher ground notion of becoming a "gateway", one of the most challenging aspects for the new corporation is to join and combine people and entities when and where needed.
5. What is needed is to be found at the critical points on the customer activity cycle – for both existing, emerging *and* imagined situations.

Any new model or representation for competitiveness must start with this.

6. Given that customers increasingly want the results (the "verbs") rather than just the goods (the "nouns"), much of the competition for customer "ownership" is likely to come from outside traditional core boundaries.
7. It's almost impossible for a single entity – be it a unit/company/country/or industry – to produce an offering that will be able to compete for customer "ownership".
8. The new corporation needs to learn how to produce integrated offerings around the customer activity cycle, with converging technologies and new working arrangements spanning old structural boundaries.
9. "Gateways" then become the powerful centre in a customer value-creating and delivery system (based on value to end-user customer) as opposed to the dominant or dominating force in a supply/distribution chain (based on volumes).
10. A leap to new customer logic requires educating not just our own people, but other members of the channel, and indeed customers who are themselves often in a state of radical transformation.

Defining New Competitive Spaces

Let's look (Table 26.1) at some of the main differences between old competitive spaces – that divided corporations into functions, tasks and jobs – and new "competitive spaces" based on resources and skills combined and recombined to add value for customers on their activity cycle.

All of these differences can be summarized by saying that new "competitive spaces" are shaped around customer activities, instead of those of the corporation.

With new customer logic, once the critical value points in the customer activity cycle have been identified, the corporation knows what needs to get done and where.

Then they work backwards to create and align delivery units to support these value points. And entities to support these delivery units.

What then distinguishes or separates one entity/company/country from another depends on how and where the customer assigns value, rather than how

Table 26.1   Old and new "competitive spaces"

Old Competitive Spaces are:	New Competitive Spaces are:
Based on structural categories (i.e. products/functions/units/companies/countries/industries)	Based on value add through the CAC
Are within set boundaries	Are without boundaries either internal or external
Built to get the best expertise into these structural categories	Built to get the best expertise (and combination) of expertise out to customers
Held together by authority and control(s)	Bonded by commitment to common customer goals, terms and tools
Cut for convenient P+L allocation and measurement	Shaped and aligned to fit customer value
Made to minimize contact and maximize independence	Formulated to maximize interdependence and connection
Encouraged to compete for resources	Expected to share resources and work with collaborative plus competitive agendas
Aimed to segregate structural categories	Aimed to disaggregate and coordinate to produce high value at low delivered cost
Based on transfer prices to maximize profit of each structural category/product portfolio	Based on reciprocity and maximizing profitability of customer/customer portfolio
Built for people to do one specific task (set of tasks)	Built for getting synergies by pulling together skills and multi-skills
Made so people have responsibility for what they can control	Made so that people have joint responsibility for customer "ownership"

corporations want to be structured to allocate, measure and control resources.

In new "competitive spaces" each and every entity either creates or delivers value, or they support someone else who does.

As part of the transformation process skills are pooled and then reclustered.

Each delivery and support entity does what they do best (this is disaggregation) so as to make units as small, specialized (and efficient) as possible.

They become, however, interdependent, because they are linked together (coordinated) into a bigger entity so as to produce the integrated customer results – on which they are now jointly judged.

Jack Welch made the idea of a "boundarylessness" organization famous, using this powerful and what was then new concept to get people to think, talk and work

Giving "Boundary-lessness" Customer Definition

together across the massive corporation, needed, he believed, to take GE through the 1990s.

Still alive and doing well at GE, "boundarylessness" has got increasingly sophisticated.

For corporations transforming today, a grounded customer logic gives "boundarylessness" an organizing frame around which resources can be mobilized and organized.

(Why, Welch asked a conference in December 1995, do 30 000 out of every million bags handled by the airlines in the US still get lost ("the same management can get *you* from a-b but not your bags"!).)

Categories like product/function/unit/company/country or industry are recombined around value adds in the CAC.

They become the new "competitive space", discovering and delivering "gateway" solutions within defined (yet ever-evolving) "market spaces".

Figure 26.1 is a visual trigger for communicating this concept, built upon our previous discussions.

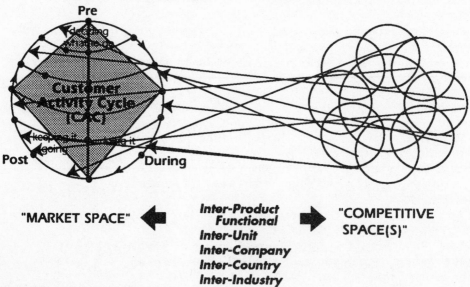

Figure 26.1 New Competitive Spaces

Creating New Geo-"Competitive Spaces"

"Competitive spaces" are increasingly cross-country as customer habits and operations – both domestic and corporate – transcend traditional physical and psychological boundaries.

Technology makes it possible to build strategies which follow customers into these new geo-"competitive spaces" instead of expecting customers to operate piece-part, dealing with unconnected corporate bits.

Some fundamentals needed to make this work:

- Global clients must be served and recognized any place worldwide, obtaining from any country what they can get from their own, and getting from one country what is applicable in their own country, and in all others (e.g. Zurich Insurance will now insure a boat bought for use in Norway for people who live in Denmark or Sweden, etc., instead of customers having to go from country to country for their insurance needs).
- The various parts of the business to which customers are exposed must be recognizable if not consistent (e.g. the look of the branch and procedures at Citibank are now the same globally).
- Differences should be based on the individual customer, rather than just country differences.
- Consistent handling, delivery and standards of quality is essential and a range of issues need to be covered by the transforming institution to achieve this, such as: how to handle different perceptions of what is and isn't good quality; the different levels of competency from country to country; costs and differences in labour laws.

We can no longer expect everyone to be good at everything or do everything – nor do we want or can we afford this.

Responsibility has to be transferred from individual countries to the new geo-"competitive spaces".

This significantly changes the role of the country and country management, who, rather than manage assets, now take on roles of ensuring effective delivery in their part of the new geo-"competitive space" in which the customer needs service.

Making New "Competitive Spaces" Virtual

Many new "competitive spaces" will be virtual.

Says Charles Handy, in his article, "Trust and the Virtual Organization" in *Harvard Business Review*, virtual spaces are inevitable today.

"Like it or not, the mixture of economics and technology means that more and more of us will be spending time in virtual space – out of sight if not out of touch."

The point is that large parts of new "competitive spaces" will contain people brought together for a particular time and purpose related to creating and delivering customer value. But they won't be permanently together, or have to sit next to each other in order to achieve this.

Virtual Geo-
"Competitive
Spaces" at 3M

At 3M getting knowledge, commitment and ideas shared and exploited across borders was always cumbersome and slow.

Energy and resources spent on duplications, waste and politics which got in the way of corporations and their customers in the past, is now replaced by harnessing efforts to produce effective products and services intercountry.

Then, recalled one 3M executive, there were difficulties when customers wanted services across Europe, because every country lived in its own reality: if a customer company wanted to, say, refurbish 5000 sites across the continent they could not have got one consistent answer, price or commitment.

What's more, distributors and dealers were buying across borders because of these inconsistencies.

New geo-"competitive spaces" – many virtual – were created around 19 European Business Centres at 3M, instead of the old country subsidiaries.

With neither project nor permanent responsibility, 21 000 people at 3M now work within these new Euro-virtual "competitive spaces" to achieve cross-border customer effectiveness. Those who need to see each other do so, talking to a boss more or less monthly at differing convenient locations.

The fact that people are not necessarily forced to physically move was a huge advantage, 3M found when it established virtual teaming in its major Europewide transformation.

Fewer than 40 managers from the European operation had to relocate.

Virtual Sales
Spaces at
AT&T

Several adjustments are needed to make virtual spaces succeed.

People must learn to work together from afar, use IT for communication, building trust cross-wire and work, without the usual physical kinds of contact and socialization needed to keep groups feeling a sense of togetherness.

Despite being in the high-tech industry themselves, corporations like AT&T have struggled with this.

This was one of the learnings for Dick Falcone, who led the sales force transformation, which took AT&T into the small business market in 1990.

On his visits to the branches one of the questions which Falcone continued to hear from his sales people was why they had to come into an office at all.

Falcone began to see that "boxing" people in physically also "boxed" in their individual aspirations and sense of accountability, as well as their competitive drive. It also led people to feel that someone down the hall either could solve their problems or would blame them for not having fixed it themselves.

That made employees focus on the internal structure, and their position in it, rather than out in the market place with customers.

Falcone began to create virtual environments in which people did not have set work places and hours, but were connected to the firm through a telecommunications network. Employees received the relevant technology and training, and branch managers were retrained on their roles, switched from "watching" to "supporting" and "coaching".

Employees decided when they worked and for how long – they set the pace and tempo, provided that results for customers were achieved (Falcone judges his sales people on how well they have "propelled" small business customers forward with better results using creative telecommunication solutions).

In forming the virtual spaces the message he gave to his staff was this: they should think and make decisions (within some clearly defined parameters) themselves, and be individually accountable for ensuring those decisions were successful.

Like everything else, people react and adapt to virtual spaces differently. Falcone found that some of the multi-thousand people didn't want to or couldn't work from home – and they remained at the office.

For others, the freedom and flexibility left them with more time and energy to be with customers, which paid off in both private and professional terms.

But what AT&T and others have learnt is that despite the inevitability and success of virtual "competitive spaces", they need to consciously eliminate the very real separation anxiety that many employees feel – they miss the social aspects of coming to work.

Falcone worked to keep regular office rituals such as lunches, meetings and other forms of exchange running, and redesigned offices to accommodate free flow and movement with people coming and going when and where they chose.

What Falcone also discovered was that a lot of the information that flowed between individuals had happened casually when they were together: when not together, a lot of this exchange and information went astray.

Experience with corporations shows that some of the time saved in virtualizing spaces must now be shifted into helping people interact with each other differently.

To provide the needed social outlets and venues for idea exchange and continued learning, people have to be consciously brought back into the organization.

Branch managers meet regularly once a week at AT&T, and branch managers and sales people are encouraged to have meetings wherever it suits – on the phone, in branch offices, homes and restaurants.

CHAPTER 27

Taking "Competitive Spaces" Across Industries

Growing market share and gaining economies of scale by acquisition and diversification. Controlling through vertical integration. These were some of the obvious strategies of the 1960s, 1970s and 1980s.

The trouble was, it made corporations bigger but not better at serving customers.

Since then we've learnt that:

What Have We Learnt?

- The offering competes, not the bits and pieces that go to make it – few of us can compete alone therefore.
- The object is to "own" the customers, not the assets or each other.
- While buyouts and/or takeovers lead to wider controls and short-term growth, ongoing competitiveness comes only from sustained market power.

As Lars Kolind from Oticon put it:

"We know we need to align more closely with our dealers and distributors to make our market impact felt. But we don't want to take over their business. We want to find a way to become a single community, sharing resources and values dedicated to the same customer 'lifelong hearing' objective."

There is a lot of talk today about strategic alliances.

With customer logic, joining forces – in whatever form that may be – makes sense only if it leads to some value or potential value add at critical points on the customer activity cycle.

Increasingly it is this that is leading corporation into new "competitive spaces" with other organizations outside their own industry.

And in time it must lead to a redefinition of industry structure and boundaries.

Can the Travel (Industry) do it?

Can the travel industry create a new competitive space?

The disconnect between the various bits of the travel experience to which I alluded in a previous chapter and which continues to plague customers, making the entire industry vulnerable, will never disappear until a new travel "competitive space" has been defined across industries.

In this model each party would take on a role to make the total customer result a joint responsibility, irrespective of who owns whom.

It is true that airlines have been collaborating for some time.

The real leap, however, is to connect the bits like travel agents, airlines, ground services, taxis hotels, etc., into a new, fully integrated "competitive space" in which everyone accepts that ultimately either everyone gains or everyone loses.

Jiffy Packaging and TNT

New "competitive spaces" have to be grown as part of the customer-driven transformation process.

It takes time and conscious effort on the part of change leaders, beginning with an awareness of the reverse customer logic, and leading to commitment to joint customer action.

An example: actualizing the obvious tie up between packaging and other industries – if value downstream was the objective – Peter Lewis made finding partners with whom to work a critical part of his transformation strategy, to turn Jiffy from a product- to a customer-driven value provider.

Partners were chosen to work on solutions in select markets.

Said Lewis:

"We chose those corporations and people within them who were receptive and open and understood what we were trying to do. It didn't matter so much whether the collaborative outcome was a formal alliance or a loose understanding provided we could find people who were the best at what they did and proactive in their thinking about customers."

With TNT, the courier/transportation corporation, Jiffy formed a "competitive space" around what the customer does to get items to and from destinations on time and in one piece.

Looking beyond specification and price, Jiffy and TNT are interested in the role of packaging/transportation solutions in the image and competitiveness of their customers.

When goods or parcels for a customer in, say, mail order, auto spare parts or PCs arrive broken or spoiled, it's not only pockets that suffer, it's also the customer's reputation.

Opinion leader customers were involved from the outset. Work has gone into assessing where the critical value adding points in the CAC exist in chosen markets and operations (such as logistics), finding the disconnects leading to the damage and loss, and jointly creating the value add solutions.

Other examples such as this one are becoming increasingly common.

New "Competitive Spaces" in Utilities

It comes from Northumbrian Water, who are testing a series of ideas in their endeavour to become the "gateway" to customer water and water-related solutions.

An experiment like the one done between themselves, British Gas and Northwestern Electric (others, e.g. telecommunications and cable will follow) in the property developer segment is destined to change not only the way utilities deal with customers, but with each other.

The challenge was as follows: how to ensure that developers got a coordinated and cost-effective service at each critical point in their CAC, without having to go from one organization to another, wasting time, effort and resources.

At the design and layout of new site pre-phase, for example, they would previously have had to send drawings to each utility separately, and each would come out with their excavation teams, dig holes, put down pipes, fill up the holes, charge, etc.

Now there is one point of contact for a single customer – someone from one of the three utilities who is appointed to coordinate activities. And the intention is to move to one billing process.

Time, energy and money are saved by the customer and, by virtue of having eliminated the duplications of effort and infrastructures, efficiencies within the newly formed "competitive space" have improved, and costs have been pulled down.

Creating a new "competitive space", based on common understanding and a common view of the world, takes top management involvement.

Dedicated resources have been allocated by the organizations mentioned to make the new initiatives work, and to show the significance both internally and in the market place.

With a view to mutual gain, new opportunities are assessed together with customers by Jiffy and TNT. For example, customer information is shared – Jiffy have launched an information service to 8000 TNT accounts on how to pack correctly so that end-users get their goods both safely and on time. Complaints to TNT on damaged products are discussed with Jiffy so that adjustments can be made and learning shared.

SECTION 11

LEARNING TO BEHAVE AS ONE

God is on the side not of the heavy battalions, but of the best shots.

Voltaire

CHAPTER 28

Altering the Way the Company Really Works

In transforming to "own" customers it's more important to create new "competitive spaces" in which skills, resources and know-how can come together and behave as one customer value-creating and delivery system, than it is to restructure corporations into new neat categories.

With a customer logic seriously under way, people quickly begin to think about new roles and ways of working, and the skills, behaviour and know-how needed to deliver value add at critical points in the customer activity cycle.

No amount of traditional restructuring will lead to the kind of fundamental deep changes in mindset and working patterns we are talking about here.

As Paul Allaire, CEO of Rank Xerox, who has personally spent a good deal of time and energy focusing on processes to achieve his new vision for the company, said:

> "There is a formal structure and then there's the way the company really works. You have to change the way it really works."

As I mentioned before, several executives who have been through or are in the process of driving their corporations to the market place, warn against restructuring, especially at the start of a customer transformation process: they say it can take energy and resources off the real issues at a very crucial time.

Given an alternate view of the world – that people understand and accept – new structures are likely to succeed.

Whereas restructuring without a solid customer base and grounding methodology makes the radical change in desired behaviour unlikely, if not impossible.

Redesigning Processes as Enablers

People like Allaire and others say that it's through a number of core processes that the way a company works ultimately gets changed.

Provided, they add, you know what it is you have to change to.

From an emphasis in the past to doing things better–faster–cheaper, the attention during the educational phase of the transformation is to enable people to achieve the dual goal of putting value in while taking non-value out.

It's about putting the tools, technology, training infrastructure and incentives in place so that people can get on and do what's neccessary, acknowledging that "the best way" can change, depending on the individual customer and circumstances.

Processes become a key enabler.

They become the connecting device for pulling the parts together, tying and uniting the various delivery entities within a "solution-based community".

And the customer activity cycles of the internal entities supporting the delivery units are linked by these new processes – all of which form the new corporate architecture.

What's a Good Process? A good processs is not just a new detailed statement of how things are now done.

In fact, the better the new processes the less need for control.

Good processes release energy, time and creative talents during a transformation, rather than inhibit or box people in.

The best processes are self-correcting and self-improving, and as such they are constantly evolving.

How to build new processes is a process in and of itself, and learning how to do that, on an ongoing basis, is part of the transformation agenda.

New corporations involve their people early on in building new processes, to get momentum flowing.

According to Les Owen this was a critical part of moving people from the initial feelings of fear to involvement, excitement and personal commitment at Sun Life Assurance.

It's about comparing what people have been recruited and trained for, and how they must now spend their time (At Sun Life they discovered that over 70% of what people had learned in the first and second years was about internal systems – nothing to do with customer value add).

Building new processes is also about helping people decide what it is they must do differently, and set themselves fresh goals.

A "straw poll" was taken of the staff – a person stationed outside the Sun Life cafeteria with a clipboard asked employees: "If you were a Sun Life customer, how long would you expect to wait to get your policy processed?" The general response given was 10 days.

The results of the poll were published and circulated throughout the company. The goal of 10 days that people came up with was far higher than management say they would have set.

Before processes are redesigned, corporations go through a period of finding out how things are currently done.

During this exercise, a lot will surface of great value if the information is creatively extracted, and the process well managed.

Important is to involve the people who do the doing in the exercise, and make sure that what comes out as "as is" is indeed representative of what goes on.

In addition to the normal process mapping techniques, involving and discussing with the people who do the doing increases the probability of getting commitment and speeding up the changes.

Northumbrian Water embarked on an interesting exercise called "A Day in the Life of . . . ". On a voluntary and confidential basis, close to 100 people across the business – from engineering to sewage operators – were closely observed.

Having all gone through customer activity cycles in previous workshops, they understood the customer mindset and gave input on what they needed to make changes – some of which they had already begun to

Building New Processes at Sun Life Assurance

Defining the "As Is"

Some Do's and
Don'ts on
Process

intitiate – happen; what barriers were still blocking them; and how they could best accomplish new customer performance.

Here are the main do's and don'ts in building new processes:

Don't:
Graft incremental improvements onto existing processes.
Do:
Let people go about doing things, as if they could start from scratch, based on a shared interpretation of customer value.

Don't:
Redesign processes to simply cut costs.
Do:
Make both putting value in *and* taking non value out, the twin objectives and processes, one of the enablers.

Don't:
Get experts in who form special teams isolated from the people who do the work, and have to make the transformation happen.
Do:
Involve as many people as you can who are in customer contact, and let them make the assessments and recommend the changes – in other words, let them tell you how they want to do it differently.

Don't:
Try to force the new organization into boxes and arrows – some of the best decisions and actions can't be "boxed in".
Do:
Start from the customer activity cycle and work back to find gaps and needed connections.

Don't:
Allow processes to be redesigned as an exercise separate from the vision, mission and new world view.
Do:
Make the new mental model, set of tools and terminology an integral part of reworking the processes.

CHAPTER 29

Learning to Jointly "Own" Customers

Independence and isolation between units and corporations become quite obviously redundant when people begin to think in terms of new "competitive spaces".

With new "competitive spaces" comes the need to:

- redefine roles and responsibilities
- assess what skills and resources are available
- reconfigurate and redeploy skills and resources, to provide the deliverables for individual customers at, and support units behind, each critical value adding point on the CAC

But, then there is the deeper challenge of getting people to feel a sense of joint customer "ownership" and mutual dependence.

Experience shows that people who have come out of traditional environments will not suddenly have a sense of mutual dependence. Nor will they instantly jump to become collaborative and interdependent.

Real efforts have to be made by change leaders to expose the barriers and articulate and implement a new set of principles and rewards.

Part of "boundarylessness" at GE is about an intellectual openness and active sharing of ideas. Whatever is learnt by the larger parts of the business is learnt by everyone.

Getting Rid of Rivalry

Said Welch in a *Financial Times* interview:

"[This] is a way of life here. People really [do] take ideas from A–B. And if you take an idea and share it, you are

rewarded. In the old culture if you had an idea you'd
keep it. Sharing it with someone else would have been
stupid, because the bureaucracy would have made him
the hero, not you."

The problem encountered is often rivalry, as Lou
Gerstner discovered when he arrived at IBM. Divisions,
he found, had been used to contention (their word),
competing not only for resources but also for customer
"ownership".
He told *Fortune*:

"We have people who will not respond to a customer
because one unit is debating with another how they're
going to share the revenue. That's ludicrous!"

The IBM group that sells PCs to schools had been told
they would have to pay royalties to the IBM PC unit if it
labelled its computer "IBM".
In an E-mail Gerstner declared: "Henceforth it will be
our policy to share with our IBM colleagues enthusias-
tically and without cost whatever we develop."
Typically in this case and others, the problem was that
several different bits of the organization were dealing
with the same customers, sometimes even offering them
identical wares.
How units were judged made them divisive: they
competed for territory, kudos, revenue – and customers.
Step one for Gerstner was trying to get the units of IBM
more closely linked to "own" key market segments.
Then, late in 1995, he pulled together the pieces of the
mammoth corporation into 11 worldwide delivery
brands in order to get focus and alignment.
People then began to seriously think about being part
of one "solution focused community", without the usual
divisional or country boundaries.

Distributing
Responsibility
at SKF

Deliberately distribute responsibilities, say some firms.
For example, SKF make each of their various
manufacturing organizations dependent upon each
other.
Each country has a pan-European responsibility for a
product line – the UK subsidiary is dependent for
instance on the French for a product needed to provide
their customers with a solution, while the French are
dependent on another product and country to fully serve
their customers.

The object of the exercise is to make each entity genuinely dependent on the other, with joint responsibility for customer outcome the goal.

To get this to work, each delivery unit must be balanced in terms of size and competence, and quality levels must be kept at the same level.

Equally, payoffs for getting it right and pain for getting it wrong must be equalized.

Sharing in the New Citibank Euro-Space

Thinking and operating effectively as one new pan-European or global "competitive space" entails a reversal in the way people think about themselves, from autonomous and separate corporate or national entities, to being part of the same value-creating and delivery system.

All the European country heads devoted to corporate customers – many of whom are fast expanding globally – meet as a team in the new Citibank 10 times or more a year for this specific purpose.

Citibank has discovered that by countries sharing resources they become closer and begin to think, talk and behave as one entity – despite cultural differences.

For example, when certain European administrative and credit processes were taken to the UK to be centralized, the team took joint responsibility for setting things up, and ensuring successful implementation and follow-through.

"The cultural problems can be overcome by moving people, having multilingual skills and so on", said one executive. "But what makes it work is the collegiality and co-venturing between the countries" (more later).

Putting New Meaning into Measures

The shift to sharing spaces and customers can't be achieved without a fundamental change in the way corporations think about and measure costs and performance.

People at 3M were judged by local results, hence the difficulty in getting enough knowledge and commitment across their domestic frontiers. Typically, remembers one 3M executive, countries would deliver for each other but like "church work in their spare time."

How we measure the contribution of the various entities, and how quickly we can change traditional measures, influences the speed at which a transformation can be implemented.

This involves changing:

• How profitability is defined, and over what time period.

- How contribution to this is calculated.
- How this contribution is recognized and rewarded.

For a variety of reasons, with new meaning in the measures, some products or country entities may not be, or may be less profitable than others at certain times.

This is OK provided their value is quantified in terms of how much they add to overall customer profitability over the longer and broader term, rather than just how much they contribute to immediate profits or corporate overheads.

Coming to
Terms With
the Numbers

Several institutions are successfully experimenting with new economics to get their organizations behaving as one thinking and operating entity.

Price Waterhouse (PW) is an example. Historically, they, like most large international corporations, had domestic accounting, computer systems, controls, evaluation and reward schemes – each country or subsidiary living in its own world.

With demand from global clients for consistent offerings across borders, P.W, like other professional service companies, have had to create new global "competitive spaces".

This has shifted them from strictly product/country economics to accounting systems based on the profitability of the customer in these new geo-"competitive spaces".

An alternative method being tried is evaluating managers on a dual system, using a two-tier P&L – one for contributions made locally and another for global/ pan European financial results.

This way, 3M say, they have been able to overcome some of the problems transforming from a domestic to a global/pan-European corporation.

Challenging
the Channel to
Become One
"Competitive
Space"

How would channels have to organize and behave if they were part of one value-creating and delivery system, as opposed to single corporations transacting with each other?

Instead of negotiating on margins or competing, benefits would have to be shared over a period of time.

Instead of telling each other as little as possible, customer information would have to be jointly collected, pooled and used.

Here is a summary of the fundamentals that need to be in place if channels are to behave as one:

1. Shared understanding of customer values and objectives – reflected in a common language and interpretation.
2. Agreement on market segments for which to aim, and value adding potential.
3. Shared resources and know-how, with transparency on restraints.
4. Common understanding of the different roles of each party contributing to customer-creating value and delivery.
5. Shared information and real time customer and learning systems.
6. Shared savings through joint elimination of duplications and waste, and controls.
7. Common performance standards, levels, measures and time frames.
8. Joint involvement in choice, training developement and evaluation of people.
9. Joint product and service research and development (R&D).
10. Open book costing, pricing and/or gain sharing, built around value for customer.

The Special Role of Trust: The DuPont Experience

"When you don't trust you have to control", said Jim Carr speaking about the new relationships DuPont Carpet Fibres have developed with manufacturers and retailers to get value add downstream to end-users.

When it discovered that homeowners in Europe had doubled their repurchase cycle time for buying new carpets to almost 12 years, and were taking 10 weeks to make a decision – reluctantly because they disliked the shopping experience so much – DuPont Carpet Fibres took the lead working with manufacturers and retailers to form a new "competitive space" with channel members for select markets.

Partners were chosen carefully and decisions taken together on end-user segments. Working in new "competitive spaces" required special attention to building trust among the various members, said Jim Carr.

"In such cases there is no substitute for face-to-face contact and discourse to get the level of trust necessary. Only through dialogue and contact do people on both sides shed their defenses."

"Openness is the only way to get the trust going that leads to commitment", says Carr.

"And sharing information that would otherwise be confidential – which we did deliberately to show both our partners and our own people that we were serious.

Most important of all is to create conditions for a genuine win/win situation and to keep doing things to reinforce it."

Between the moment an order was given to DuPont from a carpet mill and the carpet fibre was paid, several activities transpired, essentially to control each other with a lot of resulting double checking. Had the carpet fibre/ carpet arrived? Was the order correct? Had the invoice been sent? Paid?

Anything that was done essentially for administrative purposes was dropped. Firms now can bill themselves, with all savings spread and risks more than offset by gains.

The point here is that benefits must be shared.

Sharing Benefits: HP and VARS

Look at what HP has been doing.

PC street price erosion had gradually plagued distribution to such an extent that no one was really benefiting in the long term.

VARs were buying in huge quantities to get the discounts, while end-users were not really getting the services they needed to get value out of the machines.

So in 1991 HP designed the SupportPack – services in boxes, which end users would be able to touch and feel – something solid. And VARs would be able to buy, stock, store merchandise, sell and resell services like any other product.

End-users would be able to get the services either from HP or the VAR if they had the setup.

Said Alois Hauk, who led the project:

"In a collaboration, who makes the service delivery is less important than being sure end-users actually get the quality they need. We make a point not to compete with our VARs but to help them serve customers the way we would ourselves."

HP shares their administrative and IT infrastructure with VARs now. Their administrative costs of handling and reviewing contacts for SupportPack was reduced by ±30% by getting rid of non-value add activities, and renewal times were increased to get rid of further expenses. VAR costs have been pulled down by making them do as little as possible on administration and by finding ways to enable them to hold as little stock as possible.

When corporations are involved in common "competitive spaces" they will find themselves collaborating and competing simultaneously.

Organizations and the people within them need to learn to cope with the seeming contradictions this brings.

At times infrastructure, systems and cultures must be kept separate while at other times they will be fused into one.

Swiss Air, which has has had a lot of experience in this regard, emphasize the people aspects.

People who were unknown to each other have had to begin to work together and take joint responsibility for decisions and tasks for the same customers.

From one Swiss Air executive came this comment:

> "Our people had to learn that the very people they regarded as the competition were now one of them. Putting them together in one space, so they could become familiar and at ease with each other, was the first psychological step we needed to take to form one inter-company team.
>
> Getting them to talk and do things together was the second. We trained them on each other's systems and aircrafts and we deliberately got them to put each other's ideas into practice."

Collaborating and Competing Simultaneously: The Swiss Air Experience

Account management – call it what you may – has been dealt with extensively in published works over the years.

But for all the reasons we've discussed, corporations need to perfect account managing, augmenting its stature during the transformation – both internally and externally.

What account management is not is a glorified hard sell. On the contrary, many organizations struggle with whether the skills needed to sell and account manage today are possible to find in one person.

In modern corporations the account management (individual or team) is what holds together the customer relationship, especially when solutions span units/companies/industries/and countries, and coordination is needed at multiple relationship levels.

Put your best people into this role is good advice. Provided the person or team:

Account Managing as the Coordinative Force

• Knows what resources are available where

- Has access to these resources
- Has decision-making power
- Has all the relevant information
- Knows at all times what is going on between the company and the customer
- And has clout

Carr from Dupont Carpet Fibres again:

> "We tell our account managers; you and your customers take priority. No matter what the internal matter happens to be that we're dealing with, we'll drop it if you need us to see a key customer. And we do. This is our number one priority."

The move to make relationships lead to sales rather than the other way round is central to the new customer logic.

It means making sure people are incentivized accordingly.

This seems fairly obvious but often turns out to be a difficult part of the transformation process.

Partly, this is because selling on commission is so firmly entrenched in many corporate cultures. And partly because emphasis is still on producing volumes to get the numbers right.

What is the new role of selling in our organization? is a question each company will have to ask if they are to "own" their customers.

And, how would our sales people behave differently if we stopped rewarding them on volumes?

How would we judge their performance if we seriously wanted to "own" customers?

The detail of the answers will vary, but the common theme will undoubtedly be a switch in role for sales, from opening and closing deals, to creatively finding new ways of providing customers with solutions.

In new corporations, sales becomes part of the pool of resources and skills that offer expertise to customers on the customers activity cycle when and where needed.

How to measure the contribution of the sales person within the context of the entire multiple relationship then becomes the issue to tackle.

The Case of the "Case Manager" at Sun Life Assurance

Special "case managers" now handle the total relationship for customer accounts at Sun Life Assurance.

Previously, people had been recruited, trained and tooled to do one specific function inside a "box", like underwriting or administration.

Sun Life customers could have had up to 30 contact points with customers before the transformation. "Black holes", which led to delays, were due to files changing hands between departments.

On paper the sum of all the transaction time through the various departments took 20 days – but in reality customers had waited 60 days or more to get the OK.

No one had previously measured the time taken to get a life policy through the whole system – each entity was concerned about meeting their own time targets, and most did.

The new "case managers" are now responsible for all aspects of the product and customer relationship.

The object was initially to give them support through a case team – then to get them to a point where they could answer any question or take any (within broad parameters) decision impacting the customer relationship.

The principle being: they own both the problems and the solutions.

Said Les Owen:

> "All back office operations (consultants wanted to re-engineer the back office. We said; 'there are no back offices here anymore, only points of contact and support to points of contact'), have been reconfigured to support the case managers."

All checking of "case manager" work has been eliminated – leaving them free to concentrate on customers. And a system of accreditation was introduced to measure their skills as they develop.

Owen recalled:

> "As we deal in big money, we agonized over the decision to eliminate checking. We now check only 5% of all transactions – unit cost is down by 30% and speed has increased by 60%."

People who worked as checkers before were relocated to other value add activities. A decision was taken not to cut their salaries so as to reinforce new principles and behaviour.

Previous middle managers, who before were a key part of the old school culture, are now coaching and facilitating in their new roles as advisers or trainers.

Extra-
territorial
Account
Management
at IBM

Moving into global account managing, IBM introduced, and is still experimenting with, the innovative
concept of extraterritorial spaces.

An extraterritorial space is one which spans and brings
together the geographic spaces in which the customer
operates and has needs, irrespective of boundaries.

These spaces take on an identity of their own.

As in an embassy situation, where, say, the land upon
which the American embassy in Paris stands is American
territory despite being in France, this extraterritorial
space "belongs to" or, more accurately, is the responsibility of, some originating or coordinating country.

Account management is strategically placed, depending on where the high ground decisions and actions are
taken by the customer. This is fluid, so as to accommodate change.

Products and services for an oil company head-
quartered in London, for example, are managed by a
person and team in London (provided that's where
decisions are being driven from) for, say, IT.

Local providers in each country will be assigned to this
account, either exclusively or they will be involved in all
petrol companies or all UK firms operating there,
depending on circumstances.

They are responsible for their part of the global
solution delivery.

For an extraterritorial space to function, top management needs to "legitimatize" it in some appropriate way.
Though the parts are often virtual, when they operate
they must do so as one.

SECTION 12

CONVERTING INTENTION INTO VALUE

If a Man will begin with certainties he will end in doubts; but if he will be content to begin with doubts he will end in certainties.

Francis Bacon

CHAPTER 30

You Know Things are (Really) Changing When . . .

People say:

"Things feel different around here."

"I'm not afraid to speak up anymore."

"I'm spending time I never knew I had with customers."

"I'm doing new things and no one objects."

"The blockers are beginning to fall away."

"We don't have to push – ideas are now coming from the people themselves."

"We didn't get the deal but I know it's going to lead to long-term business."

"It's more difficult but I'm enjoying it more."

"I took a customer decision without having to justify or give a long explanation."

"I've got more time to attend to customers because I've let go of the controls."

"People are building tasks for themselves more challenging than anything we could have dreamed of."

"One can actually visibly see the energy level going up."

"People don't take no for an answer here anymore."

CHAPTER 31

Success as a Motivator

Change happens at different speeds in different parts of the organization – typically, most people (employees, partners and customers) look to others and their successes before they make the leap.

This is significantly different from the old days when a new book of rules was produced and sent down the organization to be obeyed.

Today we recognize that once a transformation starts, diffusion will take place through the innovators who are situated everywhere, and influence 360 degrees around themselves.

Old notions of "bottom up" or "top down" are replaced by finding the correct people and working through them, in order to make things happen, spreading the learning and and their successes, thereby building new role models.

Said one executive of a large (mature) global corporation:

> "We've learnt, you can't tell people they are wrong and expect them to change what they are doing – you have to *do it, prove it and sell it."*

How fast and how well institutionalization of new customer ways progress largely depends upon opinion leaders taking on projects which form the "pockets" (important word) of energy which pull other "pockets" along.

Projects thus become an important lever in the integration process.

Projects As Levers

Projects mobilize the innovators and opinion leaders, and act as a role model for the early and late acceptor groups.

Through them, new principles become new practice – visible, tangible and transferable.

The key to success is allocating the correct people to the projects – either fully or partly – giving them enough time out from routines for creative thinking. Also important is being clear on expectations.

Going back to Oticon for instance: once the transformation was under way a committee was formed by the "spaghetti organization" Olav Larson created, to choose the projects on which the new Oticon rested.

A member of the committee was responsible for finding a leader, who then had to form a team.

People were part of several projects. The word got round on who was making a contribution and who was overcommitted and not delivering. New performance measures were put in place for leaders of the projects, which had more to do with attracting talented people on to teams and making projects work, than having conventional type skills.

Choosing Projects That Win

An important question during the transformation is what projects to choose?

Here are some specific recommendations:

- They should be visible and do-able, so that the successes can be spread and promoted both inside the organization and in the market place.
- Early on, they should involve the correct customers and partners.
- They should be as generic as possible, so that the bulk of what is learned can be transferred – recognizing that differences are then worked out.
- They should be prioritized – not all projects will generate the same benefits or impact.

Many of the projects will be self-financing, since they will not only be creating but also extracting know-how and value.

Also some expenses will disappear as the non-value adders become redundant.

And some projects may be deliberately chosen to fund the longer-term, more costly ones.

Building "Model" Concepts

Since not everything can be done by everyone or financed all at once, firms have to build "model concepts".

A "model concept" is what it says, an ideal way of doing things. It represents the new way of working, which has been made to work and which others can then copy.

In today's world I prefer the notion of a "model concept" to a pilot test for these reasons:

1. The old pilot test is about trying something and dropping it if it fails.

Whereas the "model concept" is about actively putting resources behind a new initiative to make sure it works, learning and then making the necessary adjustments.

2. The pilot assumes that we have enough time to test things out.

The "model concept" is based on the principle of "doing and learning", to accelerate "time to market acceptance".

3. The pilot test is usually kept isolated for fear of failure.

But building a "model concept" involves getting the correct high impact people and customers involved, and making the process transparent.

4. The pilot is made to be representative of the average.

In a "model concept" people are chosen because they are different, out front, willing and able to make it work. Their successes incite and influence others.

5. Pilot tests have a definite beginning and end.

A "model concept" continues. Once begun, they develop, and the learning spills over into other projects in the organization.

6. Pilots exclude the customer – the corporation "get's it right" and then goes to market.

Part of the objective of a "model concept" is to build relationships and share the learning, which includes experimentation – doing it for and with customers.

(If a learning consortium of sorts can be formed so much the better, where both parties invest and each has some learning to gain.)

And finally, unlike pilot tests, "model concepts" become a reference source for other customers. Once successful, they can be used as a live laboratory testing ground or show-case.

Citibank's
Model
Concept
Branch

To "fix Europe" and integrate 500 scattered branches into one new "competitive space" offering customers a total financing experience, four countries in Citibank were chosen by the then head of Consumer Services, Victor Menezes – those he felt could adapt most readily and speedily.

The other countries he continued to manage in the usual way.

The country branches had always been highly decentralized, each doing its own thing, each with its own business proposition and, ironically, those with the larger networks and revenues were the most conservative of all.

One of the four countries chosen was Greece.

Tom Sisson, who had been selected to head Citibank Consumer Banks in Greece, picked a small group and set about making some visible things happen fast.

The model branch had been developed by Sisson in Chile, one of several projects initiated in New York, had initiated with a view to getting "Citibanking" implemented worldwide.

Immediately Sisson sent his people over from Greece to Chile to see it in action.

The "model branch" was not a premises or architectural issue, but rather a part of the Tao, the way Citibank was to do business with customers, navigating them through their entire banking experiences.

In retrospect, Sisson believed that the "model branch" served several specific purposes in driving the "Citibanking" implementation.

- It provided an ideal vehicle for getting customers to "see" the new company way and to try new services.
- It was a valuable place for people to experiment, observe, learn and adapt *in situ*.
- It acted as a role model for other branches and countries.
- It made the mission tangible and thus gave the global "Citibanking" vision solidarity and cohesiveness.
- It helped build consistency in the transformation process from branch to branch, country to country.

Initially small groups were put together by Tom who intended to (and did) convert all 19 Citibank branches into model branches over time.

He insisted that every experience throughout the bank system be shared. When one person or branch had a failure or success, the learning from this experience was made known to the others.

"Strategic Review Sessions" – where countries came together regularly – were deliberately set up by Menezes to transfer know-how and successes on the model branch and other projects from one country to another.

"The pan-European rollout from country to country was deliberate and conscious", recalled one executive, "even though we didn't have a pre-set plan and had to learn as we went along."

Branch managers from the countries joined in these meetings. This sped up the rollout and built networks and friendships. One branch manager elaborated:

> "It was so interesting. We really got to know each other, so when we picked up the phone for a request for one of our customers who might have been travelling, the person at the other end knew who we were, and, more importantly, wanted to help. This helped us think about being global and offering each other's customers the services and service levels they wanted."

Menezes also used the "Strategic Review Sessions" to find out how the individual countries were doing. He made a conscious decision to avoid discussing figures – that was done at separate events. Here he wanted people to talk about what they were doing and why.

Sisson had agreed early on with Menezes that his people from Greece could go with him to these "Strategic Review Sessions". This move, Sisson reflected, was also a key reason why the transformation process proceeded faster than he had anticipated.

> "We'd argue and debate and agree and my people were there listening to everything. There was total transparency – they didn't feel left out and I didn't have to interpret for them."

CHAPTER 32

Merging Customer and Employee Expectations

When corporations decide to become a "gateway" to customer solutions, the behaviour they expect from employees is very different from that of days gone by.

Table 32.1 gives some key words reflecting old and new desired behaviours.

The table speaks for itself. New desired behaviours encapsulate everything that makes an organization proactive – able to push ahead and anticipate.

The best is made of the diversity within individuals, but at the same time synergies and integration are actively sought between them, manifesting in new behaviour in the market place.

Key Words on New Desired Behaviours

Table 32.1 Old and New Desired Behaviours

Old Desired Behaviours	New Desired Behaviours
Know	Discover
Win a point	All learn something new
Protect and account	Spread and share
Agree and get consensus	Challenge and use dissensus
Repeat	Innovate
Analyse	Imagine
Duplicate	Make relevant
Predict and be predictable	Experiment and be flexible
Control	Support
Tell	Excite
Rely on discipline	Discuss and converse
Perform at job	Make a difference through skills
Be and encourage sameness	Be part of and encourage diversity

*Don't
Separate the
Thinking from
the Doing*

Thinking and doing cannot be separated in the new corporation.

Converting intention into customer value, employees need to think about what they do and why – not just obey instructions ("we (now) need their heads thinking as well as their hands working", says David Whitwam from Whirlpool).

They need to be able to do different things in often unfamiliar circumstances, meshing specialized skills with new learnings, so that new roles become achievable.

With increasing numbers in contact with customers, they have to learn how to converse with them, sense, listen, interpret and anticipate their needs.

They need to think creatively about how to take what they see, hear and experience and translate this knowledge into a tangible part of delivery.

And share with colleagues what they discover.

Taking responsibility for things over which they may have no control, they now have "bounded discretion", meaning they are free to take decisions related to getting customer results – but within set limits.

They need to be able to think about how to make this work – doing things better and differently, and, as they learn, develop both their own skills and the know-how base of the company.

They need to understand their options, the alternative methods and costs involved in each, and how to get rid of what no longer counts.

They also need to take a higher view of the organization rather than be concerned about their own (small) piece. Nonetheless, they must be the best at that one small piece they do.

They need to learn to act ever faster, yet be judged after the event for results customers (and the corporation) get not only now, but in the future.

And deal with people who are blocking change, to whom they may still technically report, pushing for and executing new mental models despite the resistance they may encounter.

And they have to work with the existing infrastructure and systems, while simultaneously themselves creating and becoming the new.

*Making the
Mental and
Emotional
Investment*

What this boils down to is that instead of just the "physical investment" in time and effort we expected from people in the past, they now must be willing and able to make a "mental investment", taking personal initiative that enables new customer logic to come alive and become operative.

Instead of telling people what they must do, the new corporation must now tell people what it expects.

Instead of telling them how to do things, it must create the context and environment and provide the enablers to help them get on and do what needs to be done.

In addition to the "mental investment", the new corporation requires an "emotional investment" from its people.

It expects them to care and be committed to the transformation. And have a strong emotional link with the corporation.

It expects them to feel differently about themselves and their realtionship with customers.

Some people quickly become the new person. Others, as we've already discussed, will, by nature, take longer.

New corporations try to get the best out of everyone – acknowledging that their role will differ at different times. They try not to separate what is good for the individual from what is good for the business.

Part of the ambiguity with which they must deal is that they are asking people to help bring about lifelong relationships with customers, when they cannot offer their employees this self same security.

Remember Maslow's hierarchy of needs? You will recall that near the bottom of his famous pyramid he put security – the need an individual has to avoid harm and feel protected at work. At the very top he put what he called "self-actualization" – the quest individuals have to seek and fulfil their own individual talents, values and goals.

The irony is that while we are asking people to operate on the top level today, developing learning and dealing with individual customers, building relationships, adapting and absorbing new ideas and methods of work, we are unable to satisfy their more basic need for security.

How can we do this is the question being asked by change leaders?

Says Jon Hargreaves of Northumbrian Water:

"It's easy to lay people off to meet costs reduction, budgets or because they've become redundant one way or another. What's difficult is making a company customer focused, taking (all) your people with you."

"Getting people's trust is almost impossible if they fear for their jobs", continues Hargreaves, who, within two years of beginning the customer transformation process, had managed to increase productivity and profits and bring down costs more than 20% with the same number of people.

The apparent paradoxes can be handled only if people feel that through the transformation both they and the company will win.

Hargreaves again:

> "If we want people to think differently about customers we have to think differently about them.
>
> If we want to have a 'contract' with every customer we need to have a 'contract' with every employee. These two should fit.
>
> We are not talking an employee contract for life in the old sense of the word, but a contract which takes our people's whole life and lifetime work into consideration, and what they need from us at different times."

Ideally, changes made in the transformation to suit new customer needs will mesh with new employee needs.

Choice is the key. "Contracts" should address individuals in the same way that we expect them to treat customers as individuals. People need a work and remuneration package that suits them instead of what is standard and applied across the board.

Making Employees Employable

Dick Falcone, who led the transformation of the sales operations at AT&T from the large to the small business market in 1990, comments on the difference between the old notion of stability and career development to that of giving people opportunities to experience and self-develop.

> "Transformation today must have customers as its driving force, but in everything done, the successful growth of individuals working in the organization is paramount.
>
> The stability corporations like AT&T used to seek and create just doesn't exist anymore.
>
> I tell my people that even if they can't make it, or even if they don't want to, they must feel that by having worked for AT&T they'll come out a better individual, and be able to sell the skills they've acquired here or wherever they like.
>
> The main thing is that people shouldn't feel that they have to stay or feel constrained in any way: if they decide to stay it's because that's best for them and for AT&T.

What we have to do is to create an environment where staying at AT&T is clearly the best option.

But above all else, our employees must feel that they are entirely free to leave: we find the people who feel that way are the most productive individuals and the ones who stay the longest.

Becoming a successful professional and fulfilled human being is the best offer any company can hope to make to its employees today."

Jack Welch is another example of an advocate for a complete reversal in the traditional company–employee contract. When employees grapple with the outside world and win, as Welch puts it, they are essentially taking over what was previously assumed to be a corporate responsibility.

In return corporations must provide opportunities for personal and professional growth, and change the implicit contract from a guarantee that they will be employed, to a commitment to training and education so that they will have "lifetime employability".

IBM, having laid off many employees during the crisis, is now tackling this issue head on through its training. Says one European executive:

"We are asking people to ensure that they will be employable with IBM and others in the future. We are giving them the support and training to do this as a conscious part of the transformation process."

CHAPTER 33

Know-How as the New Corporate Capital

Part of converting intention into value entails capturing, developing and sharing the "mindpower"-know-how in the heads of people.

This raises an interesting question:

• Do corporations know what they know?

As one manufacturing company executive said:

> "In the past, untold amounts of time and energy had been spent by people looking for or reinventing knowledge that the corporation already had. Worse still, customers were told, we didn't know, or do it, when we did know, and had been doing it for years."

Second question:

• Do they know how to capture, quantify and communicate what they know?

And third:

• Do they know how to get what is known shared?

Know-how is the only asset which grows when used and spread around. And it grows exponentially – a small amount of sharing generates a more than proportionate increase all round.

In highly competitive environments – where people want to be better than others – the "all round", obviously, becomes a problem.

Since know-how needs to be shared but cannot be protected, it must be made ever more relevant and

individualized, if corporations are to entrench themselves
with their customers.

Before, people needed to know, so they could obey and
repeat what had been established as the rule.

Now they need to know so that they can continuously
add value to delivery for customers.

We've said that during the transformation corporations
need to:

1. Identify opportunities for putting value in, and taking
   non-value out, in existing emerging and imagined
   "market spaces".

Then:

2. Decide who needs to do what, in what "competitive
   spaces" – where, when and how.

The next step is to establish:

3. Who needs to know what, when.

Which entails:

4. Assessing who knows what.
5. Finding ways to get what people need to know to
   them, from those who already know or are learning.
6. And finding and filling know-how gaps, either by
   reskilling, retooling or partnering?

Building Know-how Networks

Know-how needs to be made tangible, not only so as to
become transferable inside the corporation, but also to be
made marketable to customers.

To make know-how tangible internally means to keep:

- Capturing what we know.
- Expanding the base through ongoing learning.
- Sharing what is known.
- Growing know-how where we are short.
- And disseminating it, so that the correct people can get
  at it easily and at the correct time.

Converting intention into value means helping people
learn in real time when and where they need help, rather
than presenting them with manuals or just bringing them
into a classroom.

And helping them put their experiences back into the
system, thus constantly updating the corporation's
knowledge base.

With information technology this becomes increasingly feasible.

Which brings a corporation transforming to these questions:

7. What is the role of information in building new capabilities (the I in IT)?
8. What technology is needed (the T in IT)?

Like many others, Price Waterhouse (PW) have developed a "neural network" spanning the world, which connects its professionals dealing with global customers who, through E-mail, are now able to share information, know-how and new ideas on an instantaneous basis.

The Price Waterhouse Neural Network

Data is collected and fed into a "segment knowledge directory", a vehicle used to deal with and share information on the affairs, needs, habits and situations of individual customers worldwide.

Breakthrough ideas can be captured and shared within minutes, passed on to the segment leaders to begin a process of testing, refining and putting them into some structure and framework for global implementation.

These types of neural networks go beyond "know-how yellow pages". Instead, they are advanced learning mechanisms enabling people out there on the job to get help in real time – when and where they need it.

Customers can access data, information and ideas from agreed parts of the network. They thus become part of the input and the output.

At Zurich Insurance knowledge databases have been set up so that discussions can take place around the world between colleagues who may never have met.

Know-how Bases at Zurich Insurance

The issue or questions are listed and retrieved by someone who shares their experience or tries to provide some guidance.

Those requesting don't know who has the solution, and those replying may not even know to whom they are talking.

But everyone is expected to add to the overall pool of know-how. And they do it because it has become accepted as an integral part of the new company way.

Getting know-how shared requires conscious effort by change leaders, especially in environments in which competition and secrecy have been the ruling culture.

One Scientific Space at 3M

At 3M, technologists in more than 100 laboratories around the world work openly and easily with one another without secrecy or protectiveness, freely exchanging ideas.

Top management deliberately organized collegial networks that scientists throughout the company can tap into for advice and assistance.

Employees with similar interests meet regularly and during the company's three-day annual technology fair, they "show-case" their latest findings for their colleagues to build their expertise and personal relationships.

Knowing How to Measure Know-how

To "own" customers we need to be able to quantify the long term value of customers to us.

And quantify the long term value of us to them.

With know-how the chief contributor to customer value, knowing how to measure it becomes essential to converting behaviour into corporate capital.

What stops us?

Again the financials can (and do).

Mostly we don't yet know how to count (and show) what is not tangible and seen.

Getting the new numbers right is a long topic, not for in-depth discussion here.

But what is important to say now, however, is that when corporations create market making missions they can expect a huge component of their offering to come from the intellectual assets which produce the know-how – expertise, experience, wisdom and stories that come from people dealing with customers.

Assessing the Value to Customers

Of course, what this know-how is worth to the company depends on what it's worth to customers, either now or in the future.

Not knowing the answer to this question, corporations will fail on at least three counts.

First, they will not be able to assess how much to invest in new customer initiatives.

Second, they will continue to think of know-how as labour and therefore a cost and, trying as they must to eliminate costs, they will tend to reduce their intellectual capital.

Third, they will keep on selling time, labour and materials and inevitably get themselves back into a commodity syndrome.

Part of Jiffy's original challenge was getting customers to see the difference between buying *en masse*, to get volume discounts, (ironic because, as we said, packaging is bulky and needs to be stored), and the total costs to them, of moving goods through their activity cycle.

The wrong packaging decision, or a badly packed parcel, could cost millions in damage to say nothing of complaints, returns and other non-value activities costing a fortune in time, money and image.

Then there is the problem of transporting, lifting, carrying, offloading and so on.

Shifting customers' attention away from cost-per-metre or cost-per-ton to their total integrated costs involves knowing how to quantify the value of the solution provided within the total "competitive space", and being able to communicate this to customers.

In this case, this would include the costs of wrapping, storing, transporting, handling what's gone wrong, and the opportunity cost of not doing certain activities that would lead to a better result.

Jiffy Shows the Total Cost of Packaging

Baxter's corporate consulting unit helps key hospital clients with the planning stages of their activity cycle, as they take on the new US challenge to improve their medical and financial performance.

Baxter's system entails having each proposal submitted including a mutually defined set of metrics, to determine the value of their services to the customer.

Results are documented by the customers, and Baxter uses this to assess its own performance.

It also provides a concrete way to demonstrate to each other, and to other customers, what can be achieved.

Baxter Measures Customer Value

Zurich Insurance Australia has done some interesting work in making tangible, and placing a value on, their know-how.

This checklist comes from them and was successfully used for customers in the transportation industry:

They ask:

A Zurich Insurance Australia Checklist

1. What are the issues for that particular industry?
2. What are the issues for that individual business?
3. What is the customer·*doing* to serve its customers?
4. What could prevent that customer from *doing* what meets its customer's needs?
5. What would be the consequences of that?

6. What value would the customer ascribe to a service that would minimize the risk of not meeting its customer's needs?

Building the Corporation's Intellectual Bank

Constantly accumulating what is known and being learnt, and spreading this, is part of the ongoing process of learning that new corporations have to go through in order to build capabilities to "own" customers.

Think about these propositions:

Proposition 1: If things are always routine, we are not learning.
Proposition 2: If things are always spontaneous, we are not learning.

That know-how needs to be both spontaneous *and* routine is part of the dynamic that comes from reconfigurating the market to produce offerings which are *both* relevant and cost effective.

If we go back to the market reconfiguration model we used in Chapter 18 (Figure 18.2, page 84), you will recall that we split the market into the mass, targeted, customized and individualized parts. We said each customer offering should reflect each of these parts of the market.

Building Economies of Know-how

Know-how clearly plays a major role.

It can contribute to making offerings both relevant *and* cost effective, if corporations learn how to spread and grow their learning and experiences.

Figure 33.1 builds on the market reconfiguration model we talked about.

Looking at the figure, know-how is needed at each of the levels:

- The *routine* know-how is for the mass within markets – level 1.
- The *dedicated* is for getting into and holding on to specific target groups – level 2.
- Then know-how needs to be further *adapted* to make the offering relevant to different user groups – level 3.
- And some know-how must be *spontaneous* – developed and delivered for unique customers and their unique real time needs – level 4.

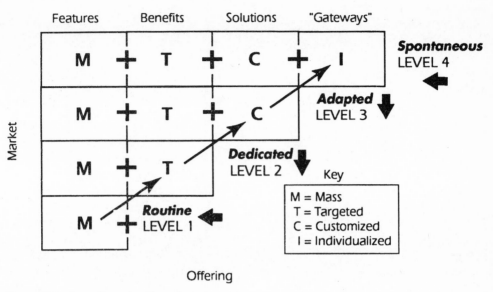

Figure 33.1   Reconfigurating Know-how

In sum, know-how that is routine must be dedicated, adapted and made spontaneous, if solutions are to become individualized. (hence the "up" arrows on the figure).

And spontaneous know-how needs to be fed back into the system, so it can be "packaged" and sold to a wider group of customers (hence the "down" arrows on the figure). This is the way the "economies of know-how" new corporations need to be competitive are created.

However, what is spontaneous cannot always be shared.

There are limits.

Either the customer is unique (a hairdresser will tell you no two heads of hair are ever the same), or corporate customers compete with each other and thus part of the know-how must be kept proprietary.

Being able to separate this out, knowing who owns what and what can be shared; being able to cater to competing customers offering them all value add; setting up "chinese walls" to protect customers without deterring from the overall worth of corporate capital, are still more paradoxes with which the new corporation will have to wrestle.

Limits to Sharing?

SECTION 13

OPERATING ON TWIN TRACKS

They must often change who would be constant in happiness or wisdom.

Confucius

CHAPTER 34

Leaping, Learning – and Leading

The Figure 34.1 joins two diagrams we have discussed in previous chapters – the S life cycle curve and the three stages of a transformation aimed at lifelong customer "ownership", namely: agitation, education and integration.

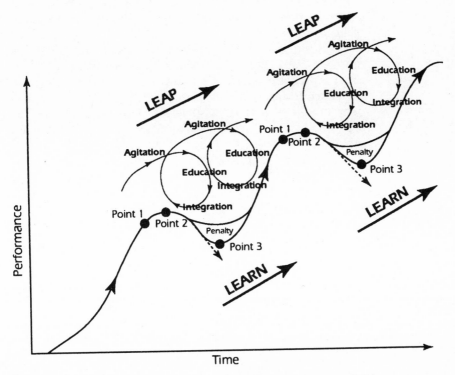

Figure 34.1 Leaping and Learning Through Transformation Stages on S Curve

Transforma-
tion Stages
Along the S
Life Cycle
Curve

The intention is to show transformation as a dynamic, ongoing, spiralling process:

- With each phase reinforcing the next, based on what's being learnt and experienced in the various parts of the organization, at varying speeds.
- And with each transformation leading to yet another on a never-ending basis.

Having made the initial leap, the new company proactively continues to learn and leap, learn and leap.

It also learns *how* to leap and how to better know when to leap – sensing, interpreting and communicating signals, translating them into new directions and opportunities.

The point is that the new corporation makes the appropriate and proactive moves at the right moment – before stagnation or crisis set in.

It becomes self-adaptive, with a capacity to renew and reshape itself, as "market spaces" emerge and expand – building continued market power in new "competitive spaces".

Activating
and
Actualizing
the Trans-
formation

No longer can corporations just repeat and get better at past experiences, they need to experiment and learn, in order to grow.

No longer can they simply respond to customer requests and that way improve performance. They must anticipate the possibilities, for and with customers.

In corporations transforming to "own" customers, key people take the risks associated with making "model concepts" work and making these a role model for others.

In the initial leap from product to market, corporation to customer, a radically different way of looking at the world is opened up by change leaders.

They change not just the corporate strategy, but the assumptions about what makes a corporation and the people within it successful.

They show that the diminishing world, in which profits were made by looking inward to figure out what goods to make and how to get them out into the market place quicker/cheaper/better than others doing the same thing, has to be reversed.

In its place a forwards–backward logic asks:

1. What do customers value, and what do we need to know how to do, in order to add value to what they

do, so as to get the results they want – now and over the period and progression of their lives.

Then:

2. What needs to be done, by whom, when and how within our organization and with others?

And:

3. How does this change what we need to be good at?

The new corporation knows it cannot transform itself in isolation.

As it changes, it changes what is around it – simultaneously finding and fuelling the future.

New institutions don't rely on survey feedback from customers to make their proactive moves – they involve and influence customers – both internal and external – and are influenced and involved by them.

They and their customers are inextricably bound up.

They create and extract value through interaction and relationships at multiple customer levels.

Like themselves, many of their corporate customers are going through transformation – so they have to learn how to be "on the move for and with others also on the move".

Rooting changes into a customer culture involves explicitly stating (and rewarding) new desired behaviours, and how and why they differ from the old.

Also, articulating the connection between new behaviours and customer successes – otherwise people quickly revert back.

New change leaders accept that though transformation must be fluid, people do need stepping stones, and there is a discernible process at work which needs to be managed.

The Transformation Phases Revisited

Challenge one is to prepare the ground, getting people to understand and accept the new world view.

Challenge two is to give them the freedom and elbow room to do what's needed by releasing time, energy and resources which create an environment, and which, together with the enablers, make customer-centred behaviour not only achievable, but sustainable.

Here are the phases summarized:

Phase 1 – agitation is when people need to be made to feel a sense of urgency and understand why the corporation needs to change its thinking, language and behaviour to fit the new customer logic.

They need to be given time to think about how they have been taught to think in the past, and how this has shaped their attitude to and actions towards customers – both internal and external.

Consciously, minds need to be opened.

Then changing minds becomes the prime task.

Phase 2 – education includes providing an alternative model (which is not only understandable but also actionable).

It's about people experimenting with and about customers, testing and implementing new ideas, based on a commonly shared interpretation of the priorities and opportunities in existing markets as well as those emerging or imagined.

A new set of tools and terminology provides a framework in which people can begin to do different things as well as do things differently.

And, importantly, build confidence in taking personal initiative, instead of experiencing the constant insecurity born of, and perpetuated by, the industrial era.

New change leaders accept that most people can and want to take new initiatives at differing speeds.

But that often they don't know how.

Also many may have long wanted to do much of what is now being advocated, but never dared, in the controlled environments in which they had had to work.

The best ideas are seeded, encouraged to grow and shared through projects, which not only build critical capabilities but do so together with customers, obtaining tangible results by doing, learning and adapting.

Good visions rooted in new customer logic expand frontiers and latitude quite naturally, and they provide perspectives, priorities and a set of principles by which people must now work.

Getting a common language helps set and gain common customer ground – everyone acknowledges that the correct moves are those which get people closer to getting close to customer.

Phase 3 is the time when sufficient people turn new insights and frameworks into behaviour, and this behaviour is made the norm.

Only when there is this distinct change from individual to corporate behaviour, has a transformation been actualized.

In making customers a lifelong investment, new corporations must place great store on the individual who learns while doing, making adjustments in real time.

Change
Without Fear

Getting it wrong is part of the process of getting it right.

Which means change leaders allow themselves and others to make mistakes rather than trying to prepare yet another book of rules to cover all customers and eventualities.

It is said that William McKnight, founder of 3M, lived by this axiom and that it is this that has made the corporation so entrepreneurial.

Mistakes would be made by people but in the long run these would not be as serious as "the mistakes management will make if it is dictatorial and undertakes to tell those under its authority exactly how they must do their jobs".

Taking the stigma out of failure and converting mistakes into learning is a deliberate part of the transformation process.

If people are afraid, or are still being "controlled" in the old mould, behaviours simply won't change.

People must feel free to share what's good and bad and challenge what is blocking their efforts.

Some organizations include feedback and learning from mistakes into employee evaluations, to solidly embody customer learning into the new culture.

Others use complaints.

Whereas before complaints were seen as flaws exposed, and the object was often to identify and punish the culprits, getting and handling complaints is now recognized as central to the lifelong learning relationship with customers.

CHAPTER 35

Living with Ambiguity

Ambiguity is a normal part of any customer-driven transformation.

This doesn't mean transformation can't be consciously managed. Only that inconsistencies along the way must be seen and communicated as a natural part of the process.

The unexpected will invariably happen.

Not surprisingly, this frightens and confuses many people.

Today's corporate leaders are having to say:

"We can give you clear direction but we don't know exactly how we are going to get there."

"There is no manual, no book of rules, no magic strategy document from the top."

"We can provide and help you discover new frameworks, ideas and tools, but you must translate them into daily behaviour."

"We can provide the resources, support and infrastructure, but you have to do the doing."

In his book *Managing with Dual Strategies*, Derek Abell, a colleague from IMD in Switzerland, discussed the fact that management as a human endeavour differs from others – in which at times we invest and at times we consume – in that running a business and changing it simultaneously are not sequential but parallel pursuits.

The Fast and Slow(er) Track

For this we need to be able to work on different tracks and balance long- and short-term goals as we go.

New change leaders work in the present and the future simultaneously.

They keep within the "sphere" of their stated vision to maintain the focus and direction of the transformation, but always with one eye stretching to horizons beyond what they can presently see.

They know they need to operate on twin tracks at different speeds, making sure that the one doesn't interfere with the corporation's ability to achieve the other.

They hear:

"You can't predict or plan" – "You must keep coming back to the basic strategy."

"Move faster than ever before" – "Go only as quickly as people can tolerate."

"Move quicker or people will revert back to old behaviour" – "There are limits to the amount of change people can tolerate."

"Do what's possible and can be done naturally well in a reasonable time frame" – "Do what's impossible, if it needs doing, no matter how long it takes."

"Keep the bonfires burning" – "There is too much change happening."

Managing the Contradictions

Change leaders have to manage these contradictions.

Working on two fronts simultaneously, they alter the pace depending on with what and with whom they are dealing.

With 36 000-odd people involved in the Zurich Insurance transformation, Rolf Huppi conscientiously managed different tracks within the different countries and parts of the business.

The fast – which he defined as the "do-able" – focused on more operational aspects, and he pushed to get these done quickly.

On the slow(er) track, initiatives, he knew, would take longer. But they had to be done to fulfil his vision.

Some corporations see more than two tracks, and explicitly state this to their people. By splitting initiatives into the different categories, they are better able to manage the various paces moving simultaneously toward the goal.

Citibank, for instance, divides projects into three categories: one, the visible high priorities which should and could be done immediately; two, those involving "stretch goals" which need more time and systematic change efforts; and three, those requiring what Citibank calls superstretch – capabilities and goals taking a longer period to accomplish.

At some moment in the integration phase of the transformation, the fast and slow(er) track(s) must converge.

While change leaders cannot manage each piece or project in the transformation – they must manage the dynamics between the pieces and projects to accomplish this.

Only they can pull them together, building bridges between the fast and the slow(er) tracks, knowing which levers to pull, with whom, when and where.

Another part of the challenge in driving a corporation to the market is this: partly decisions and initiatives will need to be chaotic and partly they will be structured.

Balancing Structure and Chaos

People who like structure become uncomfortable with the chaos, whereas others get excited and driven by it.

Modern change leaders know the difference between the two, and that there is an appropriate role and time for order as well as disorder, if the transformation is to be a journey which needs to be discovered rather than an event planned in minute detail.

They know they must balance this order and disorder, and take on the ambivalent roles that this demands – disrupting at some points to get strategic discomfort while providing stability at others.

What keeps them on track is consistency in both the message and the methods, matched by an ability and credibility that enables them to manoeuvre when needed.

Part of their challenge is being the role model themselves for the behaviour they expect from others. And making their organization into the kind they expect their customers and partners to become.

CHAPTER 36

Finding, Fuelling and Funding
the Future

Initiatives which lead to real customer transformation
don't all show quick bottom line results. Yet firms
continue to use minds and methods which are based on
the short term.

They focus on a point in time rather than demonstrat-
ing the value of and for customers over time. They
continue to ask: what will it cost now and what will be
our return now?

New corporations ask a different set of questions:

- What will it cost if we don't do it?
- What return can we get from customers over their
  lifetime, if we do it better than anyone else?
- What will this take?
- What will this cost?
- What will we lose if we don't do it?
- And what will that cost?

Here (Table 36.1) is a list of the economic questions the
new corporations needs to be able to answer:

In truth most corporations continue to judge in the
short term, because they are judged in the short term (did
you know that according to Navajo Indian folklore, a
chief cannot make a decision unless he has considered its
possible effects on seven generations hence?).

With pressure to show results quickly, get the ratios
right and watch the share price on a minute-for-minute
basis, without some alternate or supplementary way to
express what they are doing with customers, why, over
what period, to what end, corporations will continue to

Asking the
New Economic
Questions

Table 36.1 The Economic Questions

Not Just	But Also
• How do we increase market share?	• What will it take to commit the customers we want for a lifetime?
• What is the value of our customer(s) as a % of sales?	• What is the lifetime worth of our customer(s)?
• Can we cut unit cost/hold margins to maintain profitability?	• How can we better serve customers to get a deeper share of their spending?
• Are our products/services/countries/ units/companies/branches/profitable?	• Are our customers profitable?
• What are our cost of sales and services?	• What's the cost of losing a customer?
• How do we get costs down?	• What costs can we eliminate because they add no value for our customers?
• What is the cost of the activities we do?	• What is the opportunity cost of the activities we do?
• What are the unit costs of our products and services to us?	• What is the total integrated cost of our products and services to our customers?
• How do we allocate costs to products/ services/units/companies/countries/ branches?	• How do we: 1. Share resources 2. Allocate value for contribution to customer profitability?
• What will it cost to increase customer value?	• How do we increase value for customers and simultaneously decrease costs?

be caught in this short-term "capital pathology" trap aiming to please short-term investors.

New corporations know that the figures can only tell them something about their performance in the past.

They put energy into finding, fuelling and funding a sustainable future.

Like any other investment, investing in customers means accepting that a lot of the time and energy and money spent initially will take time to pay off.

At Citibank's corporate banking division, where the entire vitality of the business hinges around expanding relationships and frontiers with customers, account managers spend a good chunk of their time being with prospective customers, assessing new trends, giving them proposals and ideas before any deal is signed.

Ed Holmes, managing director of Citibank NA, says this is a very frustrating time because very little happens. He calls it "the two year tunnel".

"To get through this tunnel you have to reward people for doing the right things, even though they don't get the business immediately.

Customers may initially say: we like your ideas and your people, we see what you can do, but at the moment we don't have business for you.

You can actually feel the moment when that changes, when you start getting to the end of the tunnel and you are going to have a different life with the customer.

But you need to learn to live with the period in between if you want get on to a higher plateau with customers.

You need to take the enthusiasm and creativity people have generated and make it worth something – to them and to the organization."

An executive whom I've mentioned before by name but would now prefer to keep anonymous, recently went to his board with a proposed reduction in profits for 1996.

This is what he said to me:

"For as long as we talk one way and act another, for as long as we are trying to meet budgets, come what may, without being prepared to invest in the future, there will be no future to talk of.

I'm going to try to persuade my board to give up profits next year so that we can spend more on building up our customer relationships and finding new market opportunities.

Corporations have to make some sacrifices in the short term to make the long term a reality."

Do they dare . . . ?

References, Bibliography and Points of Departure

SECTION 1

Chapter 1

(1) As far as I know, the term "owning" the customer has not been used before. The importance of establishing "long-term" relationships with customers has, however, been discussed by numerous authors.

(2) For general reading on the subject of long-term relationships with customers, see, for instance:

M. Christopher, A. Payne and D. Ballantyne, *Relationship Marketing: Bringing Quality, Customer Service and Marketing Together*, Oxford: Butterworth Heinemann, 1991.
F. Gouillart and J. Kelly, *Transforming the Organization*, New York: McGraw Hill, 1995.
G. Heil, T. Parker and R. Tate, *Leadership and the Customer Revolution*, New York: Van Nostrand Reinhold, 1995.
M. Treacy and F. Wiersema, *The Discipline of Market Leaders*, Reading, Mass: Addison Wesley, 1995.
T. Vavra, *Aftermarketing: How to Keep Customers for Life Through Relationship Marketing*, (revised) Homewood, Illinois: Business One Irwin, 1995.
F. Webster, *Market-Driven Management: Using the New Marketing Concept to Create a Customer-oriented Company*, New York: John Wiley and Sons, 1994.

Chapter 2

(1) P. F. Drucker in *Post-Capitalist Society*, New York: Harper Business, 1993, talks about "destabilization" and the need for "creative destruction" in corporations, a term first coined by Joseph Schumpeter.

(2) Andrew Grove quotes E. Faltermayer, "Andy Grove: How Intel Makes Spending Pay Off", *Fortune*, 22 February 1993.

(3) Gates quote from his book *Bill Gates The Road Ahead*, New York: Viking, 1995, p. 64.

(4) For an interesting read on what transformation is, see B. Blumenthal and P. Haspeslagh, "Towards a Definition of Corporate Transformation", *Sloan Management Review*, Spring 1994.

(5) For general reading on corporate transformation:

J. D. Duck, "Managing Change: The Art Of Balancing", *Harvard Business Review*, November/December 1993.
C. Gersick, "Revolutionary Change Theories: A Multilevel Exploration of the Punctuated Equilibrium Paradigm", *Academy of Management Review*, January 1991.
J. Kotter, "Leading Change: Why Transformation Efforts Fail", *Harvard Business Review*, March 1995.
N. Nohria and R. Khurana, "Executing Change: Three Generic Strategies", *Harvard Business School Note*, 1993.
S. Vandermerwe and A. Vandermerwe, "Making Strategic Change Happen", *European Management Journal*, Vol. 9, No. 2, June 1991.

(6) For problems of business process re-engineering and restructuring, and corporate transformation, for example:

J. Dixon, P. Arnold, J. Heineke, J. Kim and P. Mulligan, "Business Process Reengineering: Improving in New Strategic Directions", *California Management Review*, Summer 1994.
T. Furey and S. Diorio, "Making Reengineering Strategic", *Planning Review*, July/August 1994.
M. Hammer, Interview with, *Forbes ASAP*, 13 September 1993.

J. Kotter, "Leading Change: Why Transformation Efforts Fail", *Harvard Business Review*, March 1995.
C. Lorenz, "Putting Re-engineering in Perspective", *Financial Times*, 21 October 1994.

(7) On finding triggers and transforming: P. Strebel, "Choosing the Right Change Path", *California Management Review*, Winter 1994.

(8) For more on IBM before and during the crisis, and some of the material used in this book, see:

P. Carroll, *Big Blues: The Unmaking of IBM*, London: Weidenfeld 1993.
T. Clarke and J Jaben, "IBM's Destiny: Marketing Challenge Hinges on Meeting Customer Demands"; *Business Marketing*, May 1993.
M. Dunn, "IBM Chief Warns Big Changes Needed", *Newsbytes*, 21 April 1995.
C. Ferguson and C. Morris, *The Computer Wars: The Fall of IBM and the Future of Global Technology*, New York: Random House/Times Books 1993.
S. Greyer and N. Langford, "IBM: When the Numbers Failed to Compute", *Harvard Business School Case Study*, 1993.
R. Heller, *The Fate of IBM*, New York: Little Brown & Co., 1993.
I. Jaben, "Customer Time for Big Blues", *Business Marketing*, May 1993.
Ketelhöhn W and B. Robbins, "From Big Blue to Baby Blues", *IMD Case Study*, 1994.
D. Lichtenthal and W. Copulsky, "How Big Blue Became Black and Blue", *Industrial Marketing Management*, vol. 22, 1993.
G. Lloyd and M. Phillips, "Inside IBM: Strategic Management in a Federation of Businesses", *Long Range Planning*, Vol. 27, 1994.
"Remarketing IBM – Special Report", *Business Marketing*, May 1993.
D. Yoffie and D. Pearson, "Transformation of IBM", *Harvard Business School Case Study*, 1991.
W. D. Yoffie and J. Cohn, "The Transformation of IBM – Supplement", *Harvard Business School Case Study*, 1993.

(9) For more on success inhibiting transformation, see:

D. L. Barton, *Wellsprings of Knowledge*, Cambridge: Harvard Business School Press, 1995.
M. Davidson, *The Transformation of Management*, London: Macmillan, 1995.
D. Miller, *The Icarus Paradox: How Exceptional Companies Bring About Their Own Downfall*, New York: Harper, 1990.

(10) Jack Welch quote, and general reading and information on GE used in various chapters, see:

Anonymous, "Jack Welch's Lessons for Success", *Fortune*, 25 January 1993.
R. Slater, *The New GE: How Jack Welch Revived an American Institution*, Homewood, Illinois: Business One Irwin, 1993.
N. Tichy and S. Sherman, *Control Your Destiny or Someone Else Will: How Jack Welch is Making General Electric the World's Most Competitive Corporation*, New York: Doubleday, 1993.

(11) More on Northumbrian in case study: S. Vandermerwe, "Northumbrian Water: From Monopoly Utility to Competitive Service Entity", *IMD Case Study*, 1994.

Chapter 3

(1) Points on curve adapted from original work done by J. Fry and P. Killing, *Strategic Analysis and Action*, Prentice Hall 1986, and summarized by Killing and Fry in their 1986 "Managing Change: Pace Targets And Tactics" in *IMD Perspectives (number 4)*.

(2) For an original read on the S curve and transformation, see C. Handy, *The Empty Raincoat*, London: Hutchinson, 1994.

(3) For more on organizational transformation as an evolutionary process, transformation modes and when to transform, for instance:

C. Baden-Fuller and J. Stopford, *Rejuvenating the Mature Business*, Cambridge: Harvard Business School Press, 1994.

D. Hurst, *Crisis and Renewal: Meeting the Challenge of Organizational Change*, Cambridge: Harvard Business School Press, 1995.

N. Imparato and O. Harari, *Jumping the Curve: Innovation and Strategic Choice in an Age of Transition*, San Francisco: Jossey Bass, 1994.

D. Nadler, R. Shaw and E. Walton, *Discontinuous Change: Leading Organizational Transformation*, San Francisco: Jossey Bass, 1995.

Chapter 4

(1) See J.B. Quinn, *Intelligent Enterprise*, New York: The Free Press, 1992 for a good example on problems with the current notion of market share.

(2) On getting 100% share of a redefined market, see B. Henderson, "The Origins of Strategy", *Harvard Business Review*, November 1989.

SECTION 2

Chapter 5

(1) For introductory reading on Internet and the web, see S. Levy, "This Changes Everything", *Newsweek*, 25 December 1995 and 1 January 1996.

(2) Customer satisfaction – its importance and its limits – discussed in:

E. Anderson, C. Fornell and D. Lehmann, "Customer Satisfaction, Market Share and Profitability: Findings from Sweden", *Journal of Marketing*, July 1994.

B. Gale, *Managing Customer Value*, New York: The Free Press, 1994.

T. D. Jones and E. Sasser Jr, "Why Satisfied Customers Defect", *Harvard Business Review*, November/December 1995.

S. Perkins, "Measuring Customer Satisfaction", *Industrial Marketing Management*, Vol. 22, 1993.

F. Reichheld, "Loyalty Based Management", *Harvard Business Review*, March/April 1993.

(3) Automobile figures on satisfaction/dissatisfaction from a paper by F. F. Reicheld, "The Satisfaction Trap", Bain and Company, USA: January 1993.

(4) "Sticking to the core" was a notion popularized in the book by R. Waterman and T. Peters, *In Search of Excellence*, New York: Harper & Row, 1982.

(5) More on customer long-term commitment:

J. Sviokla and B. Shapiro, *Keeping Customers*, Cambridge: Harvard Business School Press, 1993.
D. Ulrich, "Tie the Corporate Knot: Gaining Complete Customer Commitment", *Sloan Management Review*, Summer 1989.

Chapter 6

(1) For some interesting reading on the new marketing, see:

C. Grunroos, "Quo Vadis Marketing? Towards a Relationship Marketing Paradigm", *Journal of Marketing Management*, Vol. 10, No. 4 1994.
E. Gummesson, "Relationship Marketing: From 4P's to 30R's", Stockholm University Working Paper 1994.
P. Kotler, "Total Marketing", *Business Week Advance Executive Brief*, Vol. 2, 1992, and P. Kotler," Marketing's New Paradigm: What's Really Happening Out There", *Planning Review Special Issue, Conference Executive Summary*, September/October 1992.
R. McKenna, *Relationship Marketing*, Reading, Mass: Addison-Wesley, 1991.
H. Simon, "Marketing Science's Pilgrimage to the Ivory Tower", working paper O4-92, Lehrstuhl fur Betriebswirtschaftslehre und Marketing, Universitat Mainz, April 1992.

(2) B. Schlender, "What Bill Gates Really Wants", *Fortune*, 16 January 1995.

(3) More on "retention economics" and lifetime value of customers in, among others:

B. Gale, *Managing Customer Value*, New York: The Free Press, 1994.

E. Naumann and P. Shannon, "What is Customer-Driven Marketing?", *Business Horizons*, December 1992.

F. Reichheld, "Loyalty Based Management", *Harvard Business Review*, March/April 1993.

Chapter 7

See references Chapter 36 for readings on this subject.

SECTION 3

Chapter 8

(1) M. Porter, *Competitive Strategy*, New York: Macmillan, 1980 for work on the classic linear value chain.

(2) DuPont from research reported by S. Vandermerwe and M. Taishoff, in "DuPont (A): Understanding the Customer's Activity Cycle", and "DuPont (B): Alliances for Total Gain", *IMD Case Studies*, 1993.

(3) For SKF data, see S. Vandermerwe and M. Taishoff, "SKF Bearings Series: Market Orientation Through Services", *IMD Case Study*, 1990.

(4) Some information on Jiffy from the case study: by S. Vandermerwe and M. Taishoff, "Jiffy (A): Managing for Customer Orientation", and "Jiffy (B): Channel Management for Customer Orientation", *IMD Case Studies*, 1993.

(5) Some information on HP from the case study by S. Vandermerwe,"Hewlett-Packard: Distributing Services Through Multichannels", *IMD Case Study*, 1993.

Chapter 9

(1) David Whitwam quoted from "The Right Way to Go Global: An Interview with David Whitwam", *Harvard Business Review*, March/April 1994.

(2) On Grove and the Pentium crisis, see *The International Herald Tribune*, 21 December 1994.

(3) Some of the material used in this text on Oticon comes from the case study by M. Gould, R. Stanford and K. Blackmon, "Revolution at Oticon A/S: (A) Vision for a Change Competent Organization; (B) Acquiring Change Competence in a 'Spaghetti' Organization", *IMD Case Study*, 1994.

Chapter 10

(1) More on mindsets and mental models – what they are and old from new – in, for instance:

R. Ornstein and P. Ehrlich, *New World, New Mind*, New York: Simon & Schuster, 1989.
R. Pascale, *Managing on the Edge*, New York: Penguin, 1990.
T. Peters, *Liberation Management*, New York: Alfred Knopf, 1992.
P. Senge, *The Fifth Discipline*, New York: Doubleday, 1990.

SECTION 4

Chapter 11

(1) I first encountered the use of the terms "agitation", "education" and "integration" in a class given by a colleague, Christopher Parker, at IMD. To my knowledge this has not been documented by anyone.

For more on this theme, see S. Vandermerwe, "The Process of Market-Driven Transformation", *Long Range Planning*, April 1995.

"Strategic discomfort" discussed in S. Vandermerwe and A. Vandermerwe, "Making Strategic Change Happen", *European Management Journal*, Vol. 9, No. 2 June 1991.

(2) A portion of the data for Sun Life Assurance comes from research for the case study by S. Vandermerwe, assisted by B. Sutton, "Sun Life Assurance PLC: (A, B, and C) Creating Sustainable Competitive Advantage Through Services", *IMD Case Study*, 1995.

(3) More on identifying and understanding market signals in, among other sources:

V. Barabba and G. Zaltman, *Hearing the Voice of the Market: Competitive Advantage Through Creative Use of Market Information*, Cambridge: Harvard Business School Press, 1991.
G. Day, "The Capabilities of Market Driven Organizations", *Journal of Marketing*, October 1994.
G. Day, "Continuous Learning about Markets", *California Management Review*, Fall 1994.
R. Whiteley, *The Customer-Driven Company*, Reading, Mass: Business Books Ltd, 1991.

(4) For Jan Carlzon and his transformation of SAS in the 1980s, see S. Vandermerwe, "Scandinavian Airlines System (SAS) Revisited: (A) Customer Relationships Through Services in the 80s", and "SAS Revisited (B): Customer Relationships Through Services in the 90s", *IMD Case Study*, 1992.

(5) On language and transformation, see R. G. Eccles and N. Nohria, *Beyond the Hype – Rediscovering the Essence of Management*, Cambridge: Harvard Business School Press, 1992.

(6) General reading on language and perception, R. J. Stevenson, *Language, Thought and Representation*, John Wiley & Sons, 1993.

(7) Some of the material discussed in chapters on Ciba Geigy Allcomm in the case study by S. Vandermerwe and M. Taishoff, "Ciba Geigy Allcomm: Making Internal Services Market Driven – Taking the Helm (Case A) and Setting Sail (Case B)", *IMD Case Study*, 1993.

Chapter 13

(1) For Gerstner's "no vision", see "Gerstner's New Vision For IBM" *Fortune*, November 1995.

(2) More on general discussions of "vision" and transformation in:

W. Belgard, K. Fisher and S. Rayner, "Vision, Opportunity, and Tenacity: Three Informal Processes That Influence Transformation", in *Corporate Transformation*, by R. Kilman and T. Covin, San Francisco: Jossey-Bass, 1988.

J.C. Collins and J.I. Porras, "Building a Visionary Company", *California Management Review*, Vol. 37, No. 2, Winter 1995.

J. Kotter, "Leading Change: Why Transformation Efforts Fail", *Harvard Business Review*, March 1995.

N. Nohria and B. Harrington, "The Rhetoric of Change", *Harvard Business School Note*, 1994.

P.J.H. Schoemaker, "How To Link Strategic Vision to Core Capabilities", *Sloan Management Review*, Fall 1992.

N. Tichy and M. Devanna, *The Transformational Leader*, New York: John Wiley, 1986.

(3) Information on Microsoft used throughout this text from various sources including those stated elsewhere, and:

S. Caulkin, "How Gates Locked the Windows", *Fortune*, 14 June 1993; *Information Technology Focus, Financial Times* – 6 September 1995; "Bill Gates and Paul Allen Talk", *Fortune*, 2 October 1995.

L. Kehoe and P. Taylor, "Microsoft Stakes a Claim in the Internet Goldrush", *Financial Times*, 11 December 1995.

A. Sampson, *Company Man*, London: Harper Collins Publishers, 1995.

(4) AT&T mission from C. Bartlett and S. Ghoshal, "Changing the Role of Top Management: Beyond Strategy to Purpose", *Harvard Business Review*, November/December 1994.

(5) Quote from Lou Gerstner from address given by him to Comdex Computer Show, Las Vegas, November 1995.

(6) Gates quote from: B. Gates, *The Road Ahead*, New York: Viking, 1995, pp. 250–251.

Chapter 14

(1) More on mission's role in the transformation process in:

A. Campbell, "The Power of Mission: Aligning Strategy and Culture", *Planning Review*, September 1992.

A. Campbell, M. Devineare and D. Young, *A Sense of Mission*, London: Hutchinson, 1990.
A. Davies, *The Strategic Role of Marketing*, London: McGraw Hill, 1995.

(2) Some of the material used on Rank Xerox from these sources:

In-house publication, *The Document Seminar*, Revision 3, May 1994.
J. Brown, "Seeing Differently: Improving the Ability of Organizations to Anticipate and Respond to the Constantly Changing Needs of Customers and Markets – The Xerox Experience", *Marketing Science Institute Conference*, 1993.
S. Charkravarty, "Back In Focus", *Forbes*, June 1994.
R. Howard, "The CEO as Organizational Architect – An Interview with Xerox's Paul Allaire", *Harvard Business Review*, September 1992.
M. Menezes and J. Serbin, "Xerox Corp.: The Customer Satisfaction Program, A and B", *Harvard Business School Case Study*, 1994.
H. Motroni, "Xerox Company Study – A Turnaround: Putting the Customer First", *Journal of Business and Industrial Marketing*, Fall 1992.
E. Ramcharandas, "Xerox Creates a Continuous Learning Environment for Business Transformation", *Planning Review*, April 1994.
R. Walker, "Rank Xerox – Management Revolution", *Long Range Planning*, Vol. 25, 1992.

(3) Quote from G. Hamel and C. Prahalad, *Competing for the Future*, Cambridge: Harvard Business School Press, 1994, pp. 103–104.

SECTION 5

Chapter 15

(1) S. Vandermerwe, *From Tin Soldiers to Russian Dolls: Creating Added Value Through Services*, Oxford: Butterworth Heinemann, 1993.

(2) Whitwam quote from "The Right Way to Go Global: An Interview with David Whitwam", *Harvard Business Review*, March 1994.

(3) More on Bally and some material in this text from the case study by S. Vandermerwe and M. Oliff, assisted by M. Stanford and H. Bauer: "Bally S.A.: From Core Competencies to Exceeding Customer Expectations", *IMD Case Study*, 1994.

SECTION 6

Chapter 17

(1) M. Porter, in *Competitive Strategy*, (1980) discussed differentiation vs. low cost strategies, New York: MacMillan.
(2) Some of the more recent writings on segmentation and transformation:

J.-P. Deschamps and R. Nayak, *Product Juggernauts: How Companies Mobilize to Generate a Stream of Market Winners*, Cambridge: Harvard Business School Press, 1995, especially Chapters 3 and 4.
S. Rapp, *Beyond Maximarketing*, New York: Mc Graw Hill, 1993.

(3) John Reed and Citibank quote from "Citicorp Faces the World: An Interview with John Reed", *Harvard Business Review*, November 1990.

A portion of the material for this book on Citibank by S. Vandermerwe and M. Taishoff, from cases "Citibank (A): The Tao of Global Consumer Banking; Citibank (B): Implementing the Global Tao Pan-Europe and in Greece; and Citibank (C): Results in Greece", *IMD Case Study*, 1994.

Chapter 18

(1) On so-called "markets of one", see:

D. Pepper and M. Rogers, *The One-to-One Future: Building Relationships One Customer at a Time*, New York: Doubleday, 1993.

(2) For an interesting discussion of the evolution of segmentation and "markets of one", see P. Kotler, "From Mass Marketing to Mass Customization", *Planning Review*, September 1989.

(3) Information on "Variations" car leasing offer from: B. Mitchener, "In This Car Pool, Drivers Can Try Any Car, Any Time", *International Herald Tribune*, 14 September 1995.

(4) Discussions on "mass customization:

First raised by S. Davis, *Future Perfect*, Reading, Mass: Addison Wesley, 1987.
Also S. Davis and B. Davidson, *2020 Vision: Transform Your Business Today to Succeed in Tomorrow's Economy*, New York: Simon & Schuster, 1991.
J. Pine, D. Peppers and M. Rogers, "Do You Want to Keep Your Customers Forever?", *Harvard Business Review*, March 1995.
J. Pine, B. Victor and A. Boynton, "Making Mass Customization Work", *Harvard Business Review*, September 1993.
J. Pine, *Mass Customization*, Cambridge: Harvard Business School Press, 1993.

SECTION 7

Chapter 19

(1) Data for Iain Vallance views on the BT transformation from A. Dunham and M. Barry, *Unique Value: The Secret of All Great Business Strategies*, London: Maxwell Publishing, 1993.

(2) IBM data from L. Hays, "Blue Period", *Wall Street Journal*, 16 May 1994.

(3) For original work on diffusion theory, see E. Rogers, *Diffusion of Innovations*, New York: The Free Press, 1982.

(4) On general principles for getting to "opinion leaders" and "innovators" first in markets and corporations, see:

J.-P. Deschamps and R. Nayak, *Product Juggernauts: How Companies Mobilize to Generate a Stream of Market Winners*, Cambridge: Harvard Business School Press, 1995, Chapter 3.
C. Herstatt and E. von Hippel, "Developing New Product Concepts via the Lead User Method", *Journal of Product Innovation Management*, September 1992.

(5) For how this applies to transformation, see S. Vandermerwe, "Diffusing New Ideas In-House", *Journal of Product Innovation Management*, Vol. 4, 1987, and S. Vandermerwe, "The Process of Market-Driven Transformation", *Long Range Planning*, April 1995.
    Also, A. Vandermerwe, unpublished work in progress, IMD.

(6) For countries, cultures and diffusion:

C. Hampten-Turner, *Corporate Culture*, London: Piatkus, 1994.
Some of the classic work from G. Hofstede, *Cultural Consequences* – International Differences in Work-Related Values, Beverley Hills: Sage Publications, 1980.
F. Trompenaars, *Riding the Waves of Culture*, London: Nicholas Brealey Publishing, 1993.

(7) Welch quotes from R. Slater, *The New GE: How Jack Welch Revived an American Institution*, Homewood, Illinois: Business One Irwin, 1993, pp. 75–76.

SECTION 8

Chapter 22

(1) Stan Davis quote from the foreword he wrote to book by J. Pine, *Mass Customization: The New Frontier in Business Competition*, Cambridge: Harvard Business School Press, 1992, p. xi.

Chapter 23

(1) More on the customer activity cycle in S. Vandermerwe, *From Tin Soldiers to Russian Dolls: Creating Added Value Through Services*, Oxford: Butterworth Heinemann,

1993 and S. Vandermerwe, "Jumping into the Customer's Activity Cycle", *Columbia Journal of World Business*, Summer 1993.

SECTION 9

Chapter 24

(1) Some of the Baxter information in this chapter and others from:

B. Yovovich, "Partnering at its Best", *Business Marketing*, March 1992.
R. Normann and R. Ramirez, *Designing Interactive Strategy*, New York: John Wiley & Sons, 1994.
T.R.V. Davis, "The Distribution Revolution", *Planning Review*, March/April 1994.

SECTION 10

Chapter 26

(1) On new building blocks:

R. Normann and R. Ramirez, *Designing Interactive Strategy*, New York: John Wiley & Sons, 1994, and their article, R. Normann and R. Ramirez, "From Value Chain to Value Constellation: Designing Interactive Strategy", *Harvard Business Review*, July 1993.
S. Vandermerwe, "Building Seamless Service Structures: Some Whys Whats Hows", *European Management Journal*, Vol. 12, No. 3, September 1994.

(2) Quote from Welch from T. Jackson and A. Gowers, "Big Enough to Make Mistakes", *Financial Times*, 21 December 1995.

(3) C. Handy, "Trust and the Virtual Organization", *Harvard Business Review*, May/June 1995.

(4) Also on virtual spaces:

D. Birchall and L. Lyons, *Creating Tomorrow's Organization*, London: FT Pitman Publishing, 1995.

W. Davidow and M. Malone, *The Virtual Corporation: Structuring and Revitalizing the Corporation for the 21st Century"*, New York: Harper, 1992.

(5) Some 3M data for this chapter and others from:

C. Lorenz, "Here, There and Everywhere", and "Facing Up to Responsibility", *Financial Times*, respectively 10 November 1993 and 15 December 1993.
S. Ghoshal and C.A. Bartlett, "Changing the Role of Top Management: Beyond Structure To Process," *Harvard Business Review*, January/February 1995.

(6) Part of the material for AT&T from case studies by S. Vandermerwe and M. Taishoff, "AT&T (A): Focusing the Services Salesforce on Customers"; "AT&T (B): Focusing the Organization on Employees"; "AT&T (C): Employees as Customers", *IMD Case Study*, 1993.

SECTION 11

Chapter 28

(1) Allaire quote comes from C. Bartlett and S. Ghoshal, "Changing the Role of Top Management: Beyond Structure to Processes", *Harvard Business Review*, January/February 1995.

(2) For more on views and experience, Allaire and other CEOs on processes, see "Leveraging Processes for Strategic Advantage", *Harvard Business Review*, September/October, 1995.

Chapter 29

(1) Welch quote from T. Jackson and A. Gowers, "Big Enough to Make Mistakes", *Financial Times*, 21 December 1996.

(2) Gerstner quote from D. Kirkpatrick, "Gerstner's Visions for the 1990's", *Fortune*, 15 February 1995.

(3) Information on SKF partly from J.R. Galbraith and E. Lawler and Associates, *Organizing for the Future; The New*

Logic for Managing Complex Organizations, San Francisco: Jossey Bass, 1993.

(4) For more on working in a network relationship and trust, see; P. McHugh, G. Merli and W.A. Wheeler III, *Beyond Business Process Reengineering*, New York: John Wiley & Sons, 1995.

(5) For a general overview on the growing importance of trust, mutual gain and working together, see:

K. Burnett, *Strategic Customer Alliances*, London: Financial Times Publishers, 1992.
R.D. Buzzell and G. Ortmeyer, "Channel Partnerships Streamline Distribution", *Sloan Management Review*, Spring 1995.
P. Drucker, "The Post-Capitalist Executive", *Harvard Business Review*, May/June 1993.
S.C. Frey Jr and M.M. Schlosser, "ABB and Ford: Creating Value Through Cooperation", *Sloan Management Review*, Fall 1993.
F. Gouillart and J. Kelly, *Transforming the Organisation*, New York: McGraw Hill, 1995.
S. Han, D. Wilson and S. Dant, "Buyer–Supplier Relationships Today", *Industrial Marketing Management*, Vol. 22, 1993.
P. Matthysens and C. van den Bulte, "Getting Closer and Nicer: Partnerships in the Supply Chain", *Long Range Planning*, Vol. 27, 1994.
R.M. Morgan and S.D. Hunt, "The Commitment-Trust Theory of Relationship Marketing", *Journal Of Marketing* Vol. 58, July 1994.
D. Tjosvold and C. Wong, "Working With Customers: Cooperation and Competition in Relational Marketing", *Journal of Marketing Management*, Vol. 10, 1994.

For role and importance of trust in different national systems, see F. Fukuyama, *Trust*, New York: The Free Press, 1995.

(6) For global networks, read R.M. Kanter, *World Class, Thriving Locally in the Global Economy*, New York: Simon & Schuster, 1995.

(7) Extraterritorial relationships are described in S. Vandermerwe, *From Tin Soldiers to Russian Dolls: Creating*

Added Value Through Services, Oxford: Butterworth Heinemann, 1993.

(8) On global cultural teaming, see M. O'Hara-Devereaux, and R. Johansen, *Global Work – Bridging Culture Distance and Time*, San Francisco: Jossey-Bass Publishers, 1994.

SECTION 12

Chapter 31

(1) For a classic on learning organizations, see P. Senge, *The Fifth Discipline*, New York: Doubleday, 1990.

(2) Also, the learning organization and behaviour:

D.A. Garvin, "Building a Learning Organization", *Harvard Business Review*, July/August 1993.
G. Binney and C. Williams, *Leaning into the Future – Changing the Way People Change Organizations*, London: Nicholas Brealey Publishing, 1995.

(3) On people in temporary projects, see H.J. Levitt and J. Lipman-Blumen, "Hot Groups", *Harvard Business Review*, July/August 1995.

Chapter 32

(1) On not separating thinking from doing and formulation from implementation, see H. Mintzberg, *The Rise and Fall of Strategic Planning*, New York: Prentice Hall, 1994.

(2) The original Maslow theory – A. Maslow, "A Theory of Human Motivation", *Psychological Review*, January 1943 – was followed by his book, A. Maslow, *Motivation and Personality*, New York: Harper, 1954.

For a contemporary interpretation and applications of Maslow, see:

B. Schneider and D. Bowen, *Winning the Service Game*, Cambridge: Harvard Business School Press, 1995.
J. D. Duck, "Managing Change: The Art of Balancing", *Harvard Business Review*, November/December 1993.

(3) On the subject of employee expectations in a changing world, see:

J. M. Hiltrop, "The Changing Psychological Contract: The Human Resource Challenge of the 1990's", *European Management Journal*, Vol. 13, No. 3, September 1995.
A serious read from, A. Sampson, *Company Man*, London: Harper Collins Publishers, 1995.

(4) Interesting reading on top management, the individual and transformation by S. Ghoshal and C. Bartlett, "Changing the Role of Top Management: Beyond Structure to Processes", *Harvard Business Review*, January/February 1995.

(5) For transformation and balancing control and empowerment, see R. Simons, "Control in an Age of Empowerment", *Harvard Business Review*, March/April 1995.

Chapter 33

(1) More on know-how as the new capital, and also the difficulties in measuring know-how, in:

R. Crawford, *In the Era of Human Capital*, New York: Harper, 1991.
S. Davis and J. Botkin, "Coming of Knowledge-Based Business", *Harvard Business Review*, September/October 1994.
P. Drucker, "New Society of Organizations", *Harvard Business Review*, January/February 1992.
R. Glazer, "Marketing in an Information Intensive Environment: Strategic Implications of Knowledge as an Asset", *Journal of Marketing*, October 1991.
T. Hope and J. Hope, *Transforming the Bottom Line*, London: Brealey Publishing, 1995.
T.A. Stewart, "Your Company's Most Valuable Asset: Intellectual Capital", *Fortune*, 3 October 1994.
J.B. Quinn, *Intelligent Enterprise*, New York: The Free Press, 1992.

SECTION 13

Chapter 34

(1) Quote on 3M, M. Dickson, "Back to the Future", *Financial Times*, 13 May 1994.

Chapter 35

(1) The reference to Abell's work in D. Abell, *Managing With Dual Strategies: Mastering the Present, Preempting the Future*, New York: The Free Press, 1993.

(2) On ambiguity and for more on what they call "bifocal vision", see N. Imparato and O. Harari, *Jumping the Curve*, San Francisco: Jossy-Bass Publishers, 1994.

(3) On uncertainty and transformation, see M. van der Erve, *Evolution Management*, Oxford: Butterworth Heinemann, 1994.

(4) On chaos and change R.D. Stacey, *The Chaos Frontier – Creative Strategic Control for Business*, Oxford: Butterworth Heinemann, 1991.

Chapter 36

For general reading on new economic questions in Table 36.1:

(1) J. Anderson and J. Narus "Capturing the Value of Supplementary Services", *Harvard Business Review*, January 1995.

D.M. Brown and S. Laverick, "Measuring Corporate Performance", *Long Range Planning*, Vol. 27, No. 4, 1994.
R. Cooper and R.S. Kaplan, "Profit Priorities from Activity-Based Costing", *Harvard Business Review*, May/ June 1991.
A. de Meyer, *Creating Product Value, Putting Manufacturing on the Strategic Agenda*, London, *Financial Times*, 1993.
F. Gouillart and J. Kelly, *Transforming the Organisation*, New York: McGraw Hill, 1995.

R.S. Kaplan and D. Norton, "Balanced Scorecard: Measures That Drive Performance", *Harvard Business Review*, January 1992.

T. Wallance, *Customer-Driven Strategy and Winning Through Operations Excellence*, London: Oliver Wright, 1992.

J. Quinn, *The Intelligent Enterprise*, New York: The Free Press, 1992.

A. Slywotzky and B. Shapiro, "Leveraging to Beat the Odds: The New Marketing Mind-Set", *Harvard Business Review*, September 1993.

T.G. Vavra, *Aftermarketing – How to Keep Customers for Life Through Relationship Marketing*, Homewood, Illinois: Business One Irwin, 1992.

Index

Praise For
THE ELEVENTH COMMANDMENT

"An excellent exposition on how to move your company from a product-making focus to a customer-owning focus."
- ***PHILIP KOTLER,*** *S. C. Johnson & Son Distinguished Professor of International Marketing, J. L. Kellogg Graduate School of Management, Northwestern University, Evanston, Illinois, USA*

"This book is about leaps and bounds, not incremental transformation; it's about relating to ('owning') customers, not about marketing in the traditional sense of the word; and it's about how to do these things, not simply pleas for new directions. It's about real examples of companies which are actually doing something radically new and different.

Early in the book, the tone is set with a quotation from George Bernard Shaw: 'I don't believe in circumstance. The people who get on in the world are the people who get up and look for the circumstances they want, and if they can't find them, make them.'

The Eleventh Commandment is an excellent book that first and foremost asks the right questions, but importantly it also provides many right answers. The Customer Activity Cycle is the key which opens the door to a rich menu of new theory based on latest best practice. For reflective practitioners who need to link theory to practice, it's a must.

*-****DEREK F. ABELL,*** *IMD International, Lausanne, Switzerland*

"When many businesses are today going through or just been through the traumas of delayering, re-engineering or just plain taking cost out, Vandermerwe's new book *The Eleventh Commandment* opens our eyes to the exciting opportunities to really grow our business, even for those who feel they are in mature businesses.

By leading us through short easy steps, provided by concise and practical chapters, Vandermerwe guides us to the opportunities that exist beyond the battleground of the traditional supplier/buyer relationship. Unlike other strategic marketing books, she provides a real workable tool that all managers in any organization can quickly use to understand, explore and invent what a customer values most.

The tool is most powerful and almost guarantees new business when used together with the customer to explore the new 'competitive spaces'."

- **PETER LEWIS,** *Managing Director, Jiffy Packaging Company Ltd, UK.*

"In The Eleventh Commandment Sandra Vandermerwe has taken us beyond customer segmentation and through the 'gateway' into a world of customer individualization based on an in-depth understanding of what customers do and will do and not just who they are.

In so doing, she brings us face-to-face with the realities of transforming the corporation to provide spontaneously and individually tailored solutions to its customers' activities operating as a 'solution focused community' without the usual divisional or country barriers.

If there is a Twelfth Commandment it is to read this book"

— **ANTHONY TRAVIS,** *Partner, Price Waterhouse,*
Geneva, Switzerland

"...understands the vocabulary of the future; the economic model suggests direction over 'data', direction that every marketer must know....is a daring and enlightening foundation for the future

...gives clear-minded direction and unrefutable evidence of a new proof positive way to market...demonstrates what the companies that will survive the future need to know today

...guides the thinking of generations to come. Ms Vandermerwe deftly uncovers the missteps of corporations and points to realistic solutions that will last....goes beyond the 'talk' of customer-focus; it shows the depth of the new thinking, and how to succeed using it.

I want everyone who joins us to read this."

— **PATTY LYON,** *Senior Partner, Ogilvy & Mather Direct,*
New York, USA

"This is a very readable book but it's not an easy read. It's feisty and provocative and at times I felt downright uncomfortable. We're not really like that, are we? I found myself saying.

The book is centred on business transformation and how corporations can successfully transform their internal logic from what Ms Vandermerwe calls 'Linear Logic' to a new 'Customer Logic'. In this logic, businesses concentrate our efforts on increasing customer value; putting value in and taking non value out of the customers activity cycle. But it's not just theoretical it's practical and peppered with common sense examples and good practices. A 'must read' for anyone who thinks seriously about business"

— **STEVE ROGERS,** *General Manager,*
Fuji Xerox Asia Pacific Pte Ltd.

"Sandra Vandermerwe is one of the most innovative thinkers in her field of research. She has a deep insight into Services, based on her consulting work with leading companies, many of which have a global reach.
Her teaching is both innovative and practical and she has been very successful in communicating to many IBM Services executives and managers her passion for being customer driven and nurturing long term relationships. This new book gives a new understanding to the creation of value in the eyes of the customers on a sustained basis."
- **JEAN-CHARLES LEVY,** *IBM Eurocoordination, Paris, France*

"Sandra Vandermerwe is a gifted communicator. Her book consists of short readable chapters like the Readers' Digest – every point illustrated with half a dozen real-life company cases. The whole book demonstrates that she lives and breathes marketing and discusses it from every angle with every company she visits and every executive she teaches.
She identifies the major challenges facing company management today:

l Visions and missions
l Creating customer value
l Managing transformation
l Building intellectual capital

One by one she takes them on and wrestles them to the ground. This book is a tour de force – a summary of all she has learned in her 'wonderful years of learning at IMD'."
- **BERNARD TAYLOR** *Henley Management College,*
Oxfordshire, UK.

"Understanding our customers, their needs and expectations has been and continues to be a journey for our company. *The Eleventh Commandment* is the perfect travel companion by offering a rare combination of experience-based insights from leading companies and challenging new concepts on the many dimensions of building and keeping long-term customer relationships.
I am convinced that Sandra Vandermerwe's book will provide our managers with a valuable source of inspiration for moving even closer to our customers in the future."
- **ROLF HÜPPI,** *Chairman & CEO, Zurich Insurance Company,*
Zurich, Switzerland